Probability & Statistics
for Quant Interviews

Probability & Statistics for Quant Interviews

Daniel Wexler

BridgeView Recruiting

ISBN: 979-8-9995607-1-1

First Edition

This book is intended for educational purposes only. The author makes no representations or warranties regarding the accuracy or completeness of the contents of this book and assumes no responsibility for errors or omissions. The material presented does not constitute financial, investment, or trading advice.

To those aspiring to enter this field.

May curiosity guide you, persistence carry you through the difficult moments, and intellectual honesty shape the way you think about markets and risk.

Preface

When I interviewed for my first quant role, probability meant coin tosses, dice, and maybe a Poisson process if the interviewer was feeling ambitious. The hardest part was usually a twist on the birthday problem or a variant of Monty Hall. Most desks still had people who priced options off intuition and a few ruled spreadsheets. The word "data" usually meant yesterday's closing prices in a CSV file someone emailed around.

That world is gone.

Walk onto a trading floor or into a quant research pod today and you are more likely to hear a debate about regularization than about Black–Scholes assumptions. You will watch people profile Python code and tune C++ kernels. You will see models that mix $E[x]$ and $E[x \mid \text{features}]$ with as much comfort as a statistician, and you will hear acronyms from machine learning used in the same sentence as "market impact" and "execution alpha." The modern quantitative researcher sits at the intersection of several traditions that used to live in separate buildings: probability theory, statistics, computing, and market microstructure.

Yet if you strip away the buzzwords and the hardware, the common denominator is still simple. Someone asks you a question about uncertainty. You have a few minutes to think. Your answer either moves money in the right direction or it does not. Behind all the layers of infrastructure and all the gloss of sophisticated frameworks, the job still reduces to reasoning clearly under uncertainty.

That is what this book is about.

Why probability and statistics still dominate quant interviews

Over the years, I have watched the interview process change format but not essence. Whiteboards were replaced by shared online editors. Brain teasers became unfashionable. Coding challenges became standard. Case studies about trading strategies and execution pipelines became more prominent. But the backbone of almost every serious quant interview remains probability and statistics.

There are practical reasons for this. Markets are noisy. Data is limited, biased, and often dirty. Decisions are repeated, sometimes thousands of times per second. Risk is defined in terms of distributions, not single scenarios. Whether you are designing a market making strategy, calibrating a volatility surface, or assessing model risk, you are ultimately working with random variables and making inferences from samples.

A surprising number of strong candidates arrive having taken advanced courses in stochastic calculus or machine learning, but stumble on the basics. They can write down a stochastic differential equation but struggle to compute $E[X^2]$ correctly for a simple mixture distribution. They know how to run a neural network library but cannot reason through what a p value actually tells them. They have implemented a Kalman filter from a template but have trouble deriving a simple maximum likelihood estimator.

Interviewers know this. That is why they reach again and again for questions that look deceptively simple. A conditional expectation here, a variance decomposition there, a combinatorial count that hides a subtle independence assumption. An interviewer would rather see how you attack those problems than hear the names of the latest models you have used.

From pre crisis quants to the present

If you look at the history of the field, a pattern emerges.

In the 1990s, as specialized programs in quantitative finance appeared, the canonical quant was a mathematician or physicist who had discovered that stochastic calculus and spectral methods could be turned into a career on a trading floor. Pricing and hedging of derivatives dominated the agenda. Most of the questions revolved around models that tried to say something rigorous about E[payoff] and its sensitivities.

In the 2000s, technology caught up with ambition. The cost of computation dropped. Electronic trading spread. Algorithmic strategies shifted attention from individual derivative contracts to entire flows of orders. Probability and statistics moved from the back pages of pricing models to the center of strategy design. It was no longer enough to understand a closed form solution for a contract. You had to understand the distribution of your daily P&L and the statistical properties of your signals.

The crisis of 2008 exposed what happens when you combine sophisticated models with weak statistical thinking. Many tools in use at the time depended on assumptions that were rarely challenged empirically. Correlation matrices were treated as constants rather than estimates. Tail events were dismissed as "once in a thousand years," as if the data could support that claim. The post crisis era demanded something different. It rewarded quants who could ask: what is actually in our data, what is just modeled convenience, and how fragile is our conclusion to errors in estimation.

The 2010s added another layer. Big data and machine learning entered the room. Firms like WorldQuant grew by industrializing research, standardizing pipelines, and distributing the search for alpha signals globally. The typical quant now had to read both a paper on optimal execution and one on gradient boosting. But whether you were fitting a linear factor model or a complex ensemble, you still needed to ask the same old questions. What is the variance of our estimator. Are our residuals behaving as assumed. What is the effect of selection bias. How big a sample do we need for a claim to be meaningful.

Through all of these shifts, the core tools of probability and statistics never stopped being central. They only gained more applications.

Why this book exists

This book is not an encyclopedia of probability or a reference manual for statistics. You can find those elsewhere. It is a focused guide to the slice of these subjects that shows up in quant interviews and, more importantly, on the job.

I have tried to write the book I wish I had when I first made the transition from theory to practice. At that time I could prove limit theorems and manipulate measure theoretic definitions, yet I still managed to confuse myself on what exactly $E[X \mid Y]$ meant in applied terms. I could integrate a probability density, but I could not always see quickly which trick would simplify an interview problem. I had seen the central limit theorem, but I did not really understand when it was safe to lean on it for a back of the envelope estimate and when it would mislead me.

You will not find many ornate proofs here. When a proof illuminates a technique or way of thinking that often shows up in interviews, we will walk through it. When it does not, we will state the result, give intuition, and move to problems where that result earns its keep. The priority is to cultivate habits of thought that let you attack new questions under time pressure.

Those habits include recognizing structure in a problem before reaching for formulas. They include translating word problems into random variables and events with clear definitions. They include sanity checking answers using bounds, limiting cases, and simple simulations. They include knowing when an approximate argument is good enough and when the details matter.

How to read and use this book

If you are preparing for quant interviews, treat this text as a set of tools rather than as material to memorize. You will see classical topics such as conditional expectation, variance, law of large numbers, central limit theorem, regression, and hypothesis testing. None of these will be new to anyone with a standard technical education. What may be new is the emphasis on how they appear under interview conditions.

Each chapter focuses on a cluster of ideas that are frequently tested. Where possible, examples are drawn from actual interview patterns or from real tasks in quantitative research. We spend time on problems that feel close to what you will face on a whiteboard. You are encouraged to work through them with pencil and paper, or with a simple interpreter, under mild time pressure. The goal is to build fluency, not just familiarity.

If you are already working in the industry, you may still find value here, especially if your day job has drifted into software or infrastructure and you want to refresh your statistical reflexes. Many experienced quants are surprised by how rusty some core ideas feel when they are pulled away from comfortable context.

If you are a student or career switcher still deciding whether this field is for you, the problems in this book will give you a realistic taste of the intellectual side of the job. If they feel like a chore, that is useful information. If they feel like puzzles you want to keep chasing, you are in the right neighborhood.

What you will not find

You will not find a long digression on every sophisticated model used in modern finance. We will not try to cover the full theory of martingales, Lévy processes, or high dimensional statistics. Those subjects are vital in practice, but they are not where most interviews live. More importantly, you cannot improvise effectively in those areas without the foundation this book tries to solidify.

You will also not find trick problems whose only purpose is to impress with cleverness. The best interview questions are those that rely on solid fundamentals, not on obscure corner cases. When a problem does have a surprising twist, it is usually because it exposes a common misunderstanding of a basic concept. We will treat those as opportunities to deepen your intuition.

A final remark before we start

Every generation of quants believes that it is living through a period of unusual change. High frequency trading. Machine learning. Alternative data. Cloud infrastructure. The list grows longer each decade. Amid that churn, a few things are stable. One of them is that a firm will always value someone who can take a messy question about risk or return, translate it into a clear probabilistic or statistical problem, and reason through it carefully.

If you work through this book with that goal in mind, then regardless of how your interviews turn out, you will have strengthened skills that remain relevant long after today's fashionable techniques are replaced by the next wave.

Turn the page. We begin where almost every interview begins, with random variables, expectations such as $E[x]$, and the art of not getting lost in the first five minutes.

Chapter 1: Foundations of Probability for Quants

Before you start grinding interview problems, it's worth recognizing that almost every "quant puzzle" you'll see is really just a probability question wearing a thin financial disguise. Whether someone asks about the chance a trader blows up, the distribution of a strategy's P&L, or the likelihood that an apparent arbitrage is just noise, they're probing how comfortably you think in probabilistic terms. At the heart of this chapter are a few deceptively simple ideas: what outcomes are possible, how we group them into events we care about, and how we assign and update beliefs about those events. Even the most intimidating quant interview question eventually reduces to: "What can happen? How likely is it? And what changes when I learn something new?"

We start with sample spaces and events because they force you to be precise about "what the world could look like." For a coin, it's just heads or tails; for a stock, it might be all possible price paths over the next day. As trivial as it sounds, many strong candidates lose points because they implicitly change the sample space mid-solution or treat vaguely specified events as if they were crystal clear. Interviewers watch whether you mentally lay out the universe of outcomes before charging into calculations.

From there, conditional probability and Bayes-style reasoning become the workhorses of quant thinking. Almost nothing in markets is unconditional. You never care about "the probability a stock crashes," you care about "the probability it crashes given that volatility has spiked and credit spreads have widened." Conditional probabilities formalize this instinct. A trader might ask: "Given we're down 3% by noon, what's the probability we end the day below −5%?" A researcher might wonder: "Given this strategy made money during the last crisis, what's the chance that was just luck?" Underneath both questions lies the same machinery: updating beliefs as new information arrives.

Bayesian thinking, in particular, is more than an exam topic; it's a quiet engine behind many real-world decisions. When a fund evaluates a new signal, they start with a prior belief ("most backtests overstate true edge") and adjust that belief after seeing performance out of sample. One curious fact: some high-frequency firms explicitly design their execution algorithms as Bayesian updaters, continuously revising their estimate of "fair value" every time a new trade or quote appears. To an outsider, the code looks complicated. To a probabilist, it's just Bayes' rule on a nanosecond loop.

Independence is another concept that seems straightforward and is anything but in practice. Interviewers love to see whether you understand when independence holds, when it doesn't, and why it matters. Two coin flips? Independent. Two daily returns on the same stock? Probably not. Two credit defaults in the same sector during a recession? Definitely not. A sobering historical note: misjudging dependence—in particular, underestimating how likely bad events are to cluster—

played a central role in the 2008 crisis. Assumptions of near-independence in certain structured products made them look safe, right up until they weren't.

Then there's combinatorics, the counting backbone behind many of the "cute" questions: shuffling decks, arranging trades, pairing counterparties, sampling portfolios. On the surface, this can feel remote from finance, but it subtly underlies ideas like how many distinct orderings of trades could have produced an observed price path, or how many ways a basket of names can default. A fun historical tidbit: the size of the sample space for a shuffled standard deck—52 factorial—is so large that if every human who has ever lived had shuffled one deck per second since the Big Bang, the probability that two decks ever landed in the exact same order would still be effectively zero. When you price securities that depend on permutations of events, you're playing in that same combinatorial sandbox.

Throughout this chapter, you'll see finance-flavored examples—default events instead of colored balls, trading days instead of coin tosses, portfolio selections instead of lottery tickets. The goal is not to dress up elementary math, but to train your intuition in the environment you actually care about. By the end, the notation should feel like a fluent language: $P(A \mid B)$ as the natural way to phrase "given what I now know," products of probabilities as the natural consequence of independence, combinations and permutations as the obvious way to count complex possibilities. Once these foundations are second nature, the more advanced topics in later chapters—stochastic processes, risk models, option pricing—stop looking like magic and start looking like inevitable consequences of the same simple ideas laid out here.

1.1: Interview Questions

1.1.1: Question 1.1

Question: If there are two coins in a bag, one biased and one fair, and you pick a coin at random and flip it 6 times, resulting in heads every time, what is the probability that you picked the biased coin?

Answer: Let B be the event that the chosen coin is biased, and let H be the event of getting 6 heads in 6 flips. Let the probability of heads for the biased coin be p (so $P(H \mid B) = p^6$). For the fair coin, $P(H \mid \text{fair}) = (0.5)^6$. Each coin is chosen with prior probability 0.5.

By Bayes' Theorem:

$$P(B \mid H) = \frac{P(H \mid B)\,P(B)}{P(H \mid B)\,P(B) + P(H \mid \text{fair})\,P(\text{fair})}$$
$$= \frac{0.5\,p^6}{0.5\,p^6 + 0.5\,(0.5)^6} = \frac{p^6}{p^6 + (0.5)^6}.$$

1.1.2: Question 1.2

Question: Given a bag containing 5 red balls and 4 blue balls, if you draw 3 balls without replacement, what is the probability that exactly 2 are red?

Answer: The total number of ways to choose 3 balls from 9 is $C(9,3)$.

To have exactly 2 red and 1 blue, choose 2 from the 5 red and 1 from the 4 blue: favorable outcomes = $C(5,2) \cdot C(4,1)$.

Thus, the probability is

$$P(\text{exactly 2 red}) = \frac{C(5,2) \cdot C(4,1)}{C(9,3)} = \frac{10 \cdot 4}{84} = \frac{40}{84} = \frac{10}{21}.$$

1.1.3: Question 1.3

Question: If X is a continuous random variable uniformly distributed between 0 and 1, what is the probability that X is greater than 0.7?

Answer: For a uniform distribution on $[0,1]$, the probability density function is $f(x) = 1$ for $0 \leq x \leq 1$. The probability that X is greater than 0.7 is the integral of $f(x)$ from 0.7 to 1:

$$P(X > 0.7) = \int_{0.7}^{1} 1 \ dx = 1 - 0.7 = 0.3.$$

So, the probability that X is greater than 0.7 is 0.3.

1.1.4: Question 1.4

Question: A fair die is rolled twice. What is the expected value of the sum of the two rolls?

Answer: The expected value of a single fair die roll is the average of its outcomes: $E[\text{one roll}] = \frac{1+2+3+4+5+6}{6} = \frac{21}{6} = 3.5$.

By linearity of expectation, the expected value of the sum of two independent rolls is the sum of their expectations: $E[\text{sum of two rolls}] = E[\text{roll}_1] + E[\text{roll}_2] = 3.5 + 3.5 = 7$.

So, the expected value of the sum of the two rolls is 7.

1.1.5: Question 1.5

Question: If two events A and B are independent, what is the probability of A given B?

Answer: For independent events A and B, the probability of A given B is simply the probability of A. Using the definition of conditional probability, $P(A \mid B) = \frac{P(A \cap B)}{P(B)}$. Independence means $P(A \cap B) = P(A)P(B)$. Substituting, $P(A \mid B) = \frac{P(A)P(B)}{P(B)} = P(A)$, assuming $P(B) \neq 0$.

Intuition: When A and B are independent, knowing that B occurred gives no information about A, so the chance of A stays $P(A)$.

1.1.6: Question 1.6

Question: In how many ways can 3 red balls and 2 blue balls be arranged in a row?

Answer: There are 5 balls in total: 3 red (identical) and 2 blue (identical). The number of distinct arrangements is the number of permutations of 5 objects with repetitions of sizes 3 and 2. This is given by
$$\frac{5!}{3! \, 2!} = \frac{120}{6 \cdot 2} = \frac{120}{12} = 10.$$
So, there are 10 different ways to arrange the 3 red balls and 2 blue balls in a row.

1.1.7: Question 1.7

Question: If X is a random variable with $E[X] = 5$ and $\text{Var}(X) = 4$, what is $E[X^2]$?

Answer: Use the variance formula: $\text{Var}(X) = E[X^2] - (E[X])^2$.

Rearrange to solve for $E[X^2]$: $E[X^2] = \text{Var}(X) + (E[X])^2$.

Substitute the given values: $E[X^2] = 4 + 5^2 = 4 + 25 = 29$.

1.1.8: Question 1.8

Question: If X is a discrete random variable with $P(X = 1) = 0.2$, $P(X = 2) = 0.5$, and $P(X = 3) = 0.3$, what is the expected value of X?

Answer: The expected value of a discrete random variable X is computed using $E[X] = \sum x \, P(X = x)$. Here, $E[X] = 1 \cdot 0.2 + 2 \cdot 0.5 + 3 \cdot 0.3 = 0.2 + 1.0 + 0.9 = 2.1$.

So, the expected value of X is $E[X] = 2.1$.

Chapter 2: Random Variables, Distributions, and Moments

Every quantitative model of returns begins with an uncomfortable admission: the future is uncertain, and we are going to treat that uncertainty as if nature were drawing numbers from an invisible lottery machine. Those invisible draws are what we call random variables. They are the backbone of modern finance, but also its greatest source of illusion, because we frequently speak and act as if we know their rules far better than we actually do.

In return modeling, a random variable is not an abstract symbol; it is tomorrow's stock return, next quarter's portfolio P&L, or the one-day move in a yield curve factor. Some of these variables live on discrete grids—think of a credit event that either happens or doesn't, or a number of trades executed—and others take on a continuum of values, like percentage returns or log-returns. The distinction between discrete and continuous turns out to matter a great deal, because it changes how we "weigh" possibilities: we either sum over individual scenarios or integrate over a continuum. Yet behind the different mathematical machinery lies the same conceptual core: each possible outcome is assigned a probability, and together those probabilities encode our beliefs about the future.

The various distribution functions—CDF, PDF, PMF—are different lenses on this same belief structure. The cumulative distribution function quietly answers the most practical questions a risk manager ever asks: "What is the chance we lose more than 5% tomorrow?" "How likely is it that our quarterly return falls below zero?" Underneath it, the density or mass functions describe how probability is spread across outcomes, revealing whether we expect calm seas with tight clustering near the mean, or turbulent markets with fat tails and wild outliers. A striking empirical fact in finance is that while many models conveniently assume normal (Gaussian) returns, actual asset returns have heavier tails and more extreme events than the normal curve would predict. This mismatch is not a minor technicality; it is why "once-in-a-thousand-years" moves seem to happen every decade.

Expectation, variance, and the higher moments of a distribution are our attempt to condense the rich shape of uncertainty into a handful of interpretable numbers. The expected return is the center of gravity of our beliefs, the single best forecast in a mean-squared sense. Variance measures the typical size of deviations from that center, and its square root—volatility—has become the lingua franca of markets. Yet two distributions can share the same mean and variance while behaving very differently in the tails, a fact traders learn the hard way when "low-vol" strategies implode on rare but massive losses. Skewness and kurtosis, though often relegated to footnotes, describe asymmetry and tail thickness and can make or break a strategy that quietly leans into rare disasters.

Relationships between random variables are just as crucial as their individual behaviors. Covariance and correlation formalize how returns move together, and they power portfolio theory's most celebrated intuition: diversification can reduce risk without proportionally sacrificing expected return. In practice, correlations are notoriously unstable, tending to creep toward one in crises. That means the very moment we most crave diversification is when the statistical relationships we estimated in calm markets become least reliable. This fragility in correlations is not just an annoyance; it is a reminder that our random variables live in a dynamic world where regimes shift and joint behavior mutates.

Conditional expectation adds another layer of sophistication: it represents what we expect to happen given that we already know something else. A volatility forecast conditional on today's market shock, or an expected return conditional on macroeconomic indicators, is fundamentally different from an unconditional long-run average. In many models, from factor investing to risk-neutral pricing, conditional expectations are the real workhorses. They allow us to translate "if this happens, then what?" into precise quantitative statements. A curious and powerful fact is that conditional expectations themselves are random variables: as new information arrives, our forecast updates, and the conditional expectation becomes the evolving state of our knowledge.

As we explore random variables, distributions, and moments in this chapter, we will keep returning to financial returns as our guiding example. Each concept—

discreteness and continuity, CDFs and PDFs, expectation and variance, dependence and conditioning—will be framed not just as mathematical formalism, but as a lens through which we view risk and opportunity. The laws of probability will not tell us exactly what tomorrow's return will be, but they give us a disciplined language for expressing uncertainty, a way to interrogate models against data, and a toolkit for turning raw randomness into structured insight.

2.1: Interview Questions

2.1.1: Question 2.1

Question: You are evaluating a new trading signal that claims to predict whether tomorrow's return on a stock index will be positive (an "up" day). Historically, the index has an up day 55% of the time.

The signal outputs either BUY or NEUTRAL each day. Backtesting on a large sample shows: - On days that turned out to be up days, the signal said BUY 70% of the time. - On days that turned out to be down days, the signal said BUY 30% of the time.

1) If the signal says BUY today, what is the probability that tomorrow will actually be an up day?

2) A colleague ignores the 55% base rate and says, "Since the signal is correct 70% of the time on up days and 70% of the time on down days (symmetrically), the probability of an up day given BUY must be about 70%." Explain precisely why

this reasoning is wrong, in terms of conditional probabilities and base rates.

Answer: Let U = up, D = down, B = BUY. Given $P(U)$ = 0.55, $P(D) = 0.45$, $P(B \mid U) = 0.70$, $P(B \mid D) = 0.30$. By Bayes:

$$P(U \mid B) = \frac{P(B \mid U)P(U)}{P(B \mid U)P(U) + P(B \mid D)P(D)}$$
$$= \frac{0.70 \cdot 0.55}{0.70 \cdot 0.55 + 0.30 \cdot 0.45} = \frac{0.385}{0.52} \approx 0.74.$$

So given BUY, the up-day probability is about 74%.

The colleague mixes up $P(\text{signal correct} \mid \text{state})$ with $P(\text{state} \mid \text{signal})$. The 70% figures are $P(B \mid U)$ and $P(\text{NEUTRAL} \mid D)$, but the trading decision needs $P(U \mid B)$. Bayes' rule multiplies likelihoods by base rates: $P(U \mid B) \propto P(B \mid U)P(U)$. Ignoring $P(U) = 0.55$ is equivalent to wrongly assuming $P(U) = P(D) = 0.5$, which changes the posterior. The asymmetric base rate (55% vs 45%) pushes $P(U \mid B)$ above 70%, to 74%.

2.1.2: Question 2.2

Question: A quant researcher models the (unknown) true expected daily excess return of a trading strategy, denoted by θ (in basis points), as a random variable. Before seeing any data, her prior is: $\theta \sim N(0, 4)$, so prior mean 0 bps and prior variance 4 (i.e., prior standard deviation 2 bps).

Each day she observes a noisy signal X_t: X_t = θ + ε_t, where ε_t are i.i.d. $N(0, 9)$ (so observation noise standard deviation is 3 bps), independent of θ.

1) After observing one day's signal X_1 = 3, what is the posterior distribution of θ? (Give its mean and variance; an explicit numeric answer is expected.)

2) After observing a second day X_2 = 3 (same realization again, independent conditional on θ), what is the new posterior mean? Without re-deriving from scratch, explain intuitively why the posterior mean moves less from day 1 to day 2 than it did from prior to day 1.

3) Suppose instead the first day was X_1 = 3 and the second day was X_2 = −3. Qualitatively (no arithmetic required), is the posterior mean after two days closer to 0 than after just the first day? Explain the intuition using Bayesian weighting of conflicting evidence.

Intuition: This is a standard normal–normal Bayesian updating problem. The posterior mean is a precision-weighted average of prior mean and observed data. Each new observation adds information (precision). Early observations move beliefs more because the prior is relatively "weak"; as variance shrinks, each additional point has smaller marginal impact, and conflicting points partially cancel each other out.

Solution: Prior is

$$\theta \sim N(\mu_0, \sigma_0^2), \quad \mu_0 = 0, \ \sigma_0^2 = 4,$$

likelihood

$$X_t \mid \theta \sim N(\theta, \sigma^2), \quad \sigma^2 = 9.$$

For one observation $X_1 = x_1$, posterior variance and mean are

$$\sigma_1^2 = \frac{1}{\frac{1}{\sigma_0^2} + \frac{1}{\sigma^2}}, \quad \mu_1 = \sigma_1^2 \left(\frac{\mu_0}{\sigma_0^2} + \frac{x_1}{\sigma^2} \right).$$

Compute variance:

$$\sigma_1^2 = \frac{1}{\frac{1}{4} + \frac{1}{9}} = \frac{1}{\frac{9+4}{36}} = \frac{36}{13} \approx 2.77.$$

Compute mean with $x_1 = 3$:

$$\mu_1 = \frac{36}{13}\left(0 + \frac{3}{9}\right) = \frac{36}{13} \cdot \frac{1}{3} = \frac{12}{13} \approx 0.92 \text{ bps.}$$

So after one day,

$$\theta \mid X_1 = 3 \sim N\left(\frac{12}{13}, \frac{36}{13}\right).$$

After a second observation $X_2 = 3$, we treat the day-1 posterior as the new prior:

$$\theta \sim N(\mu_1, \sigma_1^2).$$

Update again:

$$\sigma_2^2 = \frac{1}{\frac{1}{\sigma_1^2} + \frac{1}{\sigma^2}} = \frac{1}{\frac{13}{36} + \frac{1}{9}} = \frac{1}{\frac{13}{36} + \frac{4}{36}} = \frac{36}{17},$$

$$\mu_2 = \sigma_2^2\left(\frac{\mu_1}{\sigma_1^2} + \frac{X_2}{\sigma^2}\right) = \frac{36}{17}\left(\frac{12/13}{36/13} + \frac{3}{9}\right) = \frac{36}{17}\left(\frac{12}{36} + \frac{1}{3}\right)$$

$$= \frac{36}{17}\left(\frac{1}{3} + \frac{1}{3}\right) = \frac{36}{17} \cdot \frac{2}{3} = \frac{24}{17} \approx 1.41 \text{ bps.}$$

The move from prior to day 1 is about 0.92; from day 1 to day 2 is only about 0.49. Intuitively, the first observation dominates a diffuse prior. After updating once, the posterior variance is smaller, so the posterior already has higher precision. A new single noisy observation has less relative precision than the current belief, so its impact on the mean is weaker.

If instead $X_1 = 3$ and $X_2 = -3$, the two likelihoods pull in opposite directions. The prior is centered at 0. One positive and one negative signal of equal size and equal noise partially cancel, so the combined evidence is "less directional." Bayesian weighting of these symmetric, conflicting signals yields a posterior mean that is closer to 0 than after only seeing $X_1 = 3$, because the second observation pulls the mean back toward the prior center rather than reinforcing it.

Common Mistake: Candidates often forget that the posterior mean is not the sample average but a precision-weighted average of prior and data. They may incorrectly think identical signals always shift the mean by the same absolute amount each time, ignoring the fact that posterior variance shrinks and thus each additional observation has diminishing marginal influence.

2.1.3: Question 2.3

Question: A risk manager monitors a portfolio whose daily P&L distribution depends on whether the market is in a "low-vol" or "high-vol" regime.

Let R be the random daily P&L (in millions). Let $S \in \{L, H\}$ denote the volatility regime: L = low-vol, H = high-vol.

Model: $P(S = H) = 0.2, P(S = L) = 0.8$. Conditional on $S = L$, $R \sim N(0,1)$. Conditional on $S = H$, $R \sim N(0,4)$.

A new intraday indicator I is observed before the close. It is noisy but informative about S: $P(I = \text{"spike"} \mid S = H) = 0.9, P(I = \text{"spike"} \mid S = L) = 0.1$.

1) If you observe I = "spike", what is $P(S = H \mid I =$ "spike")?

2) Given I = "spike", compute $\text{Var}(R \mid I =$ "spike").

3) Conceptually, why does observing I = "spike" strictly increase your estimate of $\text{Var}(R)$ compared to the unconditional $\text{Var}(R)$? Identify the key probabilistic mechanism.

Intuition: There are two volatility regimes with different variances. The indicator is more likely to show "spike" when the regime is high-vol. Seeing a spike should make you more confident you are in the high-vol state, thus raising your forecast variance, because your posterior weighting on the high-variance regime increases.

Solution:

Let $H = \{S = H\}$, $L = \{S = L\}$, and $J = \{I =$ "spike"$\}$.

1) By Bayes' rule:
$$P(H \mid J) = \frac{P(J \mid H)P(H)}{P(J \mid H)P(H) + P(J \mid L)P(L)}$$
$$= \frac{0.9 \cdot 0.2}{0.9 \cdot 0.2 + 0.1 \cdot 0.8} = \frac{0.18}{0.26} \approx 0.6923.$$

2) We know
$$\text{Var}(R \mid S = L) = 1, \quad \text{Var}(R \mid S = H) = 4,$$
and $E[R \mid S] = 0$ in both regimes. Conditional on S, the indicator I does not change R's distribution, so
$$\text{Var}(R \mid S, J) = \text{Var}(R \mid S), \quad E[R \mid S, J] = 0.$$

Using the conditional law of total variance:

$$\mathrm{Var}(R \mid J) = E[\mathrm{Var}(R \mid S,J) \mid J] + \mathrm{Var}(E[R \mid S,J] \mid J)$$
$$= E[\mathrm{Var}(R \mid S) \mid J] + 0.$$

Thus

$$\mathrm{Var}(R \mid J) = 4 \cdot P(H \mid J) + 1 \cdot P(L \mid J)$$
$$= 4 \cdot 0.6923 + 1 \cdot 0.3077$$
$$\approx 2.7692 + 0.3077 \approx 3.0769.$$

3) Unconditionally,

$$\mathrm{Var}(R) = E[\mathrm{Var}(R \mid S)] + \mathrm{Var}(E[R \mid S])$$
$$= 0.2 \cdot 4 + 0.8 \cdot 1 + 0 = 1.6.$$

After observing "spike", $P(H \mid J)$ increases from 0.2 to about 0.69, so the probability weight on the high-variance regime jumps. Since total variance is the probability-weighted average of regime variances, this Bayesian reweighting toward the high-vol state strictly increases the conditional variance.

Common Mistake: Candidates often try to add some "extra" variance term from the indicator itself or forget that $E[R \mid S]$ is zero in both regimes, incorrectly keeping the second term in the law of total variance. The only effect of I is to change the posterior probabilities of the regimes, not the within-regime variance formula.

2.1.4: Question 2.4

Question: A bank uses a stress-warning model to flag days with an unusually high probability of a large negative move (say, daily loss worse than −5%). On any given day: - The true probability that such a crash day occurs is 0.5%. - The model issues a WARNING or NO WARNING. -

Historical validation shows: • P(WARNING | crash) = 0.9.
• P(WARNING | no crash) = 0.05.

1) On a day when the model issues a WARNING, what is the probability that the day is actually a crash day?

2) A manager claims: "The model is great: it detects 90% of crashes and is wrong only 5% of the time on normal days. So if it says WARNING, we're almost certainly in trouble." Quantitatively explain why this intuition is misleading, and relate your explanation to the base rate of crashes.

3) Suppose the bank's capital allocation rule is: if P(crash | WARNING) > 50%, cut risk by half; otherwise, do nothing. Based on your calculation, does this rule react too aggressively, too weakly, or about right to the WARNING signal? Justify briefly.

Answer: Using Bayes, P(crash | WARNING) = [0.9 · 0.005] / [0.9 · 0.005 + 0.05 · 0.995] ≈ 0.0829, about 8.3%. The manager confuses P(WARNING | crash) and P(WARNING | no crash) with the posterior P(crash | WARNING), neglecting the base rate P(crash) = 0.005. Because crashes are very rare, the 5% false-warning rate applied to 99.5% normal days generates many more false alarms than true ones; hence most WARNING days are non-crashes, and "almost certainly in trouble" is wrong.

The 50% threshold rule is too weak: the signal raises crash risk from 0.5% to 8.3% (about 16×), yet the bank does nothing, ignoring a large relative jump in tail risk.

2.1.5: Question 2.5

Question: You are comparing two competing models for a daily equity-return signal S_t used to predict tomorrow's excess return R_{t+1}.

Model A (no signal): $R_{t+1} \sim N(0,1)$ always.

Model B (signal matters): With probability 0.5, $S_t = 0$ and $R_{t+1} \sim N(0,1)$. With probability 0.5, $S_t = 1$ and $R_{t+1} \sim N(\mu, 1)$ with unknown $\mu > 0$.

Priors: $P(A) = P(B) = 0.5$. Under B, $\mu \sim \text{Exp}(\lambda = 2)$ with density $f(\mu) = 2e^{-2\mu}$ for $\mu > 0$.

Observation: $S_t = 1$, $R_{t+1} = x = 0.8$.

Tasks: 1) Compute $L_A = f_A(R_{t+1} = 0.8)$. 2) Given $S_t = 1$, compute $L_B = f_B(R_{t+1} = 0.8 \mid S_t = 1)$ by integrating out μ. 3) Express $P(B \mid D)$ in terms of L_A, L_B and decide if data favors B over A; explain intuitively.

Intuition: Model A insists returns are always standard normal with mean 0. Model B allows that on signal days ($S_t = 1$), the mean can be a positive μ, but μ is shrunk toward 0 by the exponential prior. Seeing $S_t = 1$ and a positive return close to 0.8 makes a model that can shift its mean upward more plausible than a fixed-zero-mean model, even after penalizing large μ.

Solution:

1) Under Model A, $R \sim N(0,1)$, so at $x = 0.8$,

$$L_A = f_A(x) = \frac{1}{\sqrt{2\pi}} \exp\left(-\frac{x^2}{2}\right) = \frac{1}{\sqrt{2\pi}} \exp\left(-\frac{0.8^2}{2}\right)$$

$$= \frac{1}{\sqrt{2\pi}} e^{-0.32}.$$

2) Under Model B with $S_t = 1$, we have $R \mid \mu \sim N(\mu, 1)$ and $\mu \sim \text{Exp}(2)$. The marginal likelihood is

$$L_B = f_B(x \mid S_t = 1) = \int_0^\infty f(x \mid \mu) f(\mu) \, d\mu$$

$$= \int_0^\infty \left[\frac{1}{\sqrt{2\pi}} e^{-\frac{(x-\mu)^2}{2}} \right] [2e^{-2\mu}] d\mu.$$

So

$$L_B = \frac{2}{\sqrt{2\pi}} \int_0^\infty \exp\left(-\frac{(x-\mu)^2}{2} - 2\mu \right) d\mu.$$

Expand the exponent:

$$\frac{(x-\mu)^2}{2} = \frac{\mu^2 - 2x\mu + x^2}{2},$$

hence

$$-\frac{(x-\mu)^2}{2} - 2\mu = -\frac{\mu^2}{2} + x\mu - \frac{x^2}{2} - 2\mu$$

$$= -\frac{\mu^2}{2} + (x-2)\mu - \frac{x^2}{2}.$$

Thus

$$L_B = \frac{2}{\sqrt{2\pi}} e^{-x^2/2} \int_0^\infty \exp\left(-\frac{\mu^2}{2} + (x-2)\mu \right) d\mu.$$

This is a Gaussian-type integral on $[0, \infty)$; for interview purposes, this level of simplification is adequate.

3) With equal model priors,

$$P(B \mid D) = \frac{L_B P(B)}{L_A P(A) + L_B P(B)} = \frac{L_B}{L_A + L_B},$$

and similarly

$$P(A \mid D) = \frac{L_A}{L_A + L_B}.$$

The data favors Model B over A if and only if $L_B > L_A$.

From the expressions,

$$L_A = \frac{1}{\sqrt{2\pi}} e^{-x^2/2}, \quad L_B = \frac{2}{\sqrt{2\pi}} e^{-x^2/2} \int_0^\infty \exp\left(-\frac{\mu^2}{2} + (x-2)\mu\right) d\mu,$$

so

$$\frac{L_B}{L_A} = 2 \int_0^\infty \exp\left(-\frac{\mu^2}{2} + (x-2)\mu\right) d\mu.$$

For $x = 0.8$, the exponent is $-\mu^2/2 - 1.2\mu$, which is negative but the integral over $\mu > 0$ is strictly positive. Numerically this ratio exceeds 1, so $L_B > L_A$ and therefore $P(B \mid D) > 0.5$.

Common Mistake: Candidates often forget to condition on $S_t = 1$ when forming L_B, incorrectly averaging over both $S_t = 0$ and $S_t = 1$. Others plug in a "best" μ (like $\mu = x$) instead of integrating over its prior, thereby ignoring the Bayesian marginal likelihood that properly balances fit and prior penalty.

2.1.6: Question 2.6

Question: You are modeling daily P&L X (in % of capital) for a high-frequency strategy. Empirically, small moves look roughly Gaussian, but you also observe occasional very large losses that are far more frequent than a normal distribution would predict.

You consider two candidate models for X: - Model G (Gaussian): X ~ N(0, 1^2). - Model T (Student-t): X ~ t_v

with mean 0 and scale chosen so that Var(X) = 1, for some
ν > 2.

1) For ν > 2, both models can be scaled to have Var(X)
   = 1. Explain why, despite having the same variance,
   the tail risk of large losses (say $P(X < -5)$) can be
   dramatically different between Model G and Model
   T.

2) Suppose your risk committee only cares about 1-
   day 99% VaR (a quantile) and not about variance.
   Argue, using properties of higher moments or tail
   behavior, which model is more appropriate to use
   for VaR estimation in this setting, and why
   matching variance alone is a poor criterion.

3) Give a concrete example (no numbers required) of
   how two distributions can have the same mean and
   variance but lead to very different qualitative risk
   assessments for a trading strategy.

Answer: For ν > 2, both distributions can have $Var(X) =$
1, but their tails decay differently. Gaussian tails decay like
$\exp(-x^2/2)$, while Student-t tails decay polynomially,
about $|x|^{-(ν+1)}$. Polynomial decay is much slower, so
$P(X < -5)$ can be many orders of magnitude larger under
the t model than under the Gaussian, despite identical
variance. Variance captures average squared deviations,
not the specific shape of extreme tails.

For 99% VaR, the far left tail matters. A heavy-tailed t with
higher kurtosis better reflects empirically frequent
extremes and yields a more conservative VaR. Matching

only variance ignores kurtosis and tail decay, which primarily drive high-quantile losses.

Example: Distribution A: $X \sim N(0,1)$. Distribution B: a mixture with mean 0 and overall variance 1, where with probability 0.99, X is tightly distributed (small variance), and with probability 0.01, X has very large variance. Both share mean and variance, but B admits occasional huge losses, implying far higher tail risk and a very different trading risk profile than A.

2.1.7: Question 2.7

Question: You model daily returns of two stocks, R_A and R_B, using a single latent market factor F and idiosyncratic noise terms ε_A, ε_B:

R_A = β_A F + ε_A, R_B = β_B F + ε_B.

1) Under these assumptions, derive Var(R_A), Var(R_B), Corr(R_A, R_B).
2) Explain conceptually why regime-switching in F raises unconditional Corr(R_A, R_B).
3) Explain why a joint Gaussian with same mean/var/corr misstates joint tail risk.

Answer: Under the single-Gaussian factor, $\text{Var}(R_A) = \beta_A^2 \sigma_F^2 + \sigma_A^2$, $\text{Var}(R_B) = \beta_B^2 \sigma_F^2 + \sigma_B^2$, and $\text{Corr}(R_A, R_B) = \beta_A \beta_B \sigma_F^2 / \left(\sqrt{\beta_A^2 \sigma_F^2 + \sigma_A^2} \sqrt{\beta_B^2 \sigma_F^2 + \sigma_B^2} \right)$.

Intuition: With regime-switching, rare stressed days have large $|F|$, so both R_A and R_B move together strongly, dominating covariance and raising unconditional correlation relative to a single Gaussian with the same $\text{Var}(F)$. The unconditional joint distribution becomes a mixture of bivariate Gaussians, which is non-Gaussian with heavier, more correlated tails. A fitted joint Gaussian matching only means, variances, and correlation ignores this mixture structure and higher moments, thus underestimates probabilities of simultaneous large losses (e.g., both $< -5\%$).

2.1.8: Question 2.8

Question: A researcher models a daily trading signal S and next-day return R as follows. Conditional on S, the return is normal: $R \mid S \sim N(S, 1)$, and S itself is random with $S \sim N(0, \tau^2)$. Assume S and the conditional noise are independent.

1) Compute $E[R]$ and $Var(R)$ in terms of τ^2 using the law of iterated expectations and the law of total variance. (You should obtain simple closed-form expressions.)

2) Interpret $Var(R)$ in terms of two intuitive sources of uncertainty in this model. Explain what each component represents in a financial context.

3) Suppose τ^2 is very large. Qualitatively, what does that say about the distribution of R and about the usefulness of the signal S for predicting R? Contrast this with the case τ^2 very close to zero.

Answer: Using iterated expectations, $E[R] = E[\,E[R \mid S]\,]$ $= E[S] = 0$. For the variance, $Var(R) = E[Var(R \mid S)] +$ $Var(E[R \mid S]) = E[1] + Var(S) = 1 + \tau^2$. The "1" is irreducible noise in returns given the signal (unpredictable market shocks). The "τ^2" is variation in expected returns due to the signal itself; it measures how much $E[R \mid S]$ moves with S. If τ^2 is very large, R is very spread out and most variability comes from predictable signal-driven shifts, so S is highly useful. If $\tau^2 \approx 0$, $R \approx N(0,1)$ regardless of S, so almost all variation is pure noise and S is nearly useless for prediction.

2.1.9: Question 2.9

Question: Consider a simple one-day payoff X (in % of notional) from a strategy that buys an out-of-the-money call option on an index. The index's one-day return R is modeled (for simplicity) as a symmetric, mean-zero distribution with finite variance and no skewness.

The strategy payoff is: $X = \max(R - k, 0)$, where $k > 0$ is the option's strike expressed as a return threshold.

1) Without doing detailed integrals, argue qualitatively why $E[X] > 0$ even though $E[R] = 0$ and the strategy only takes non-negative payoffs.

2) Compare the skewness of X to that of R. Is X left-skewed, right-skewed, or symmetric? Provide an intuitive argument based on the shape of the payoff function.

3) Suppose you form a portfolio $P = -c + X$, where $c = E[X]$ under the pricing measure (ignoring discounting), so that $E[P] = 0$. Explain why even though P has zero mean, many risk metrics based only on variance might understate its risk relative to a symmetric zero-mean asset with the same variance. Connect your answer to higher moments and the distributional shape of P.

Answer: Since R is symmetric with mean 0, there is positive probability that $R > k$. On those states, $X = R - k > 0$; otherwise $X = 0$. With no negative values and some strictly positive ones, the average payoff must satisfy $E[X] > 0$.

R is symmetric, but $X = \max(R - k, 0)$ collapses all $R \leq k$ to a point at 0 and keeps only large positive outcomes. Thus X has a point mass at 0 plus a long right tail and no left tail: it is strongly right-skewed.

For $P = -c + X$ with $E[P] = 0$, most days $R \leq k$, so $X = 0$ and $P = -c$ (frequent small loss). Rarely, $R \gg k$, so P is a large gain. This "lottery" profile has high positive skewness and fat right tail. A symmetric asset with the same variance spreads risk more evenly. Variance ignores skewness and kurtosis, so it understates how often you lose and how concentrated gains are in rare extreme events.

2.1.10: Question 2.10

Question: You are modeling the waiting time T (in trading days) until the next large market crash... [full text as given].

Intuition:

The key object is the hazard rate: "given no crash so far, how risky is the next instant?" The exponential model says the world is memoryless: risk per unit time is constant, no matter how long it has been since the last crash. The Pareto-type model is heavy-tailed, so extreme long waits are much more likely; its hazard is not flat and encodes how risk changes with elapsed time. Same mean $E[T]$ does not mean same risk story: one can be tightly concentrated, the other dominated by rare, enormous waiting times.

Solution:

For Model E, $T \sim \text{Exp}(\lambda)$, survival is

$$P(T > t) = e^{-\lambda t}, \quad f_E(t) = \lambda e^{-\lambda t}.$$

The hazard rate is

$$h_E(t) = \frac{f_E(t)}{P(T > t)} = \frac{\lambda e^{-\lambda t}}{e^{-\lambda t}} = \lambda.$$

So $h_E(t)$ is constant. Conditional crash risk in the next short interval is the same immediately after a crash and after a long quiet period.

For Model P, survival is

$$P(T > t) = \left(1 + \frac{t}{\alpha}\right)^{-\beta}, \quad t \geq 0.$$

The density is

$$f_P(t) = \frac{d}{dt}\left[1 - \left(1 + \frac{t}{\alpha}\right)^{-\beta}\right] = \frac{\beta}{\alpha}\left(1 + \frac{t}{\alpha}\right)^{-(\beta+1)}.$$

The hazard rate is

$$h_P(t) = \frac{f_P(t)}{P(T > t)} = \frac{\frac{\beta}{\alpha}\left(1 + \frac{t}{\alpha}\right)^{-(\beta+1)}}{\left(1 + \frac{t}{\alpha}\right)^{-\beta}} = \frac{\beta}{\alpha + t},$$

which strictly decreases in t. Under this specification, surviving longer actually makes the instantaneous crash risk smaller than at the start.

For part 1, exponential: flat hazard, stationary perceived risk. Pareto-type here: decreasing hazard, "if we've gone a long time without a crash, we're in a calm regime, so today is safer."

For part 2, your data say that after a very long quiet period, the probability of a crash in the next month is higher than it was right after the last crash. That corresponds to an increasing hazard with t. Model E is impossible (hazard is fixed), and the specific Pareto form above has decreasing hazard, also opposite to the data. However, among the two classes, only the non-exponential heavy-tailed family can even allow non-constant hazards; so a heavy-tailed, non-exponential model (conceptually like P, but with increasing hazard) is more consistent than E. Exponential is definitively ruled out by the observation.

For part 3, both models can be calibrated so $E[T]$ matches. For the Pareto-type, mean is finite if $\beta > 1$, but variance is finite only if $\beta > 2$; for $1 < \beta \leq 2$, $\mathrm{Var}(T) = \infty$ despite finite $E[T]$. Intuitively, in the exponential world, waiting times fluctuate around the mean and extremely long gaps are exponentially rare, so long-run crash timing is relatively predictable. In the heavy-tailed world with possibly infinite variance, a few extremely long calm periods and occasional clusters dominate the experience; the same "average waiting time" hides enormous uncertainty about when crashes actually materialize. In risk management, using a heavy-tailed model means planning for much more volatile timing of systemic events, even if the mean frequency is unchanged.

Common Mistake:

A common error is to focus only on matching $E[T]$ and to interpret that as "the models imply the same crash risk," ignoring the hazard shape and higher moments. Another mistake is to assume "heavy tail" automatically means increasing hazard; here the simple Pareto form has a decreasing hazard, so heavy tail and hazard monotonicity are logically separate issues.

Chapter 3: Core Distributions in Quant Finance

If you listen carefully to most quant interviews, beneath the brainteasers and rapid-fire math you'll hear the same quiet rhythm: a handful of probability distributions showing up over and over again, disguised in different suits. Whether the question is about default events, order arrivals, option prices, or time between trades, the interviewer is really asking: do you recognize the distribution hiding here, and do you know what to do with it?

At one extreme lies the Bernoulli distribution, the coin flip of quantitative finance. Will this counterparty default this year: yes or no? Will a limit order fill before the close: did it happen or not? In practice, entire portfolios of such "yes/no" risks are modeled as collections of Bernoulli variables, and many credit risk models start from nothing more exotic than stacked coin flips with correlations. Interviewers often sneak this in through deceptively simple questions: "Suppose a strategy wins 55% of the days; what's the chance you're profitable after 20 days?" Underneath is the Bernoulli repeated until it becomes something richer.

That "something richer" is often the Binomial distribution, which tracks how many successes you accumulate across those repeated Bernoulli trials. The iconic binomial tree for pricing options, for example, is just repeated up-or-down

Bernoulli moves for the stock price. The continuous-time Black–Scholes world is introduced as a limit of that binomial world as the time steps become finer and finer. In an interview, a candidate who can see that "number of up moves in n steps" is binomial immediately unlocks closed-form probabilities and can quickly approximate distributions, compute tail risks, or argue about convergence to the normal.

When the events become rare but possibly numerous—defaults across a gigantic bond universe, the number of trades per minute in a liquid stock, or the arrival of large orders in an electronic limit order book—the Poisson distribution steps in. Here, the randomness is in how many events occur within a given horizon. If someone asks, "If trades arrive at an average rate of five per second, what is the chance we see no trades in the next half second?", they are really checking if you spot the Poisson structure. A curious fact is that under mild assumptions, aggregating many independent Bernoulli events with tiny probabilities, but huge populations, converges to a Poisson count. This Poisson limit is why "rare events in large populations" is practically synonymous with Poisson in the quant's mental toolbox.

Layered beneath both binomial and Poisson is the question of timing. How long until the next default? Until the next market order? Until a stop-loss gets triggered by a jump? The Exponential distribution appears here as the canonical "memoryless" waiting time: the probability you must wait another hour doesn't depend on how long you've already waited. This property, unrealistic in strict detail but shockingly convenient analytically, underpins continuous-time Markov models of default, order arrivals, and jumps. Interviewers love sneaking in the memoryless trick: "If the expected waiting time is 10 minutes, what is the probability we wait more than 20?" The candidate who instantly answers without integrating anything has recognized the exponential lurking beneath.

Eventually, though, no quant can avoid the monarch of distributions: the Normal. Day-by-day P&L swings, factor returns, PCA residuals, and the theoretical log-returns in Black–Scholes are all modeled as Gaussian. Linear combinations of many small independent shocks tend, by the central limit theorem, to look normal—even if no single piece is. That one result explains why the Normal distribution is everywhere in risk modeling and portfolio theory. In interviews, Gaussian assumptions appear not only in direct form ("What's the probability of a 3-sigma loss?") but subtly, in questions about correlation, conditional expectations, or PCA: all are almost effortless once you recognize the multivariate normal structure in the background.

Yet the prices we see on screens are not normally distributed—they are strictly positive, and their relative changes compound multiplicatively. This is where the Lognormal distribution enters, describing variables whose logarithm is normal. Under the Black–Scholes framework, stock prices at a future time are lognormal, which keeps them strictly positive while still allowing the log-returns to be Gaussian and mathematically tractable. Many interview puzzles around options, volatility smiles, or "What is the distribution of S(T) if log-returns are normal?" are quietly testing whether candidates can navigate the normal–lognormal bridge without hesitation.

What makes these distributions especially powerful in interview settings is how they interlock. A Bernoulli aggregated over time becomes Binomial; with extreme scaling it becomes Poisson. Poisson waiting times are Exponential. Sums of many independent influences drift toward Normal. Exponentials of normal variables become Lognormal. Virtually any clever puzzle—about rare events, large numbers, portfolio losses, or option payoffs—reduces to one of these families once you strip away the finance story.

A strong quant doesn't just memorize formulas; they develop a kind of distributional pattern recognition. Hear "count of events in time" and think Poisson. Hear "time until next event" and think Exponential. Hear "sum of many small risks" and think Normal. Hear "price that must stay positive" and think Lognormal. In the pages that follow, we will explore not only the mathematics of these core distributions but also the tricks, approximations, and interview-style puzzles that turn them from abstract formulas into the working language of quantitative finance.

3.1: Interview Questions

3.1.1: Question 3.1

Question: A risk team monitors a daily crash-warning model for an equity index. Historically: - True crash probability on any given day is 0.1%. - If a crash will occur tomorrow, the model flashes an alarm with probability 80%. - If no crash will occur, the model still flashes a (false) alarm with probability 5%.

(a) Given an alarm today, what is the probability that a crash actually occurs tomorrow?

(b) Now suppose volatility regimes matter. On any given day, the market is either in a **high-vol regime** (H) with probability 20% or a **normal-vol regime** (N) with probability 80%. Conditional on regime:

- In H: crash probability is 0.4%, alarm true-positive is 90%, false-positive is 10%.

- In N: crash probability is 0.025%, alarm true-positive is 60%, false-positive is 3%.

Your colleague says: "If we see an alarm, we should assume we're in the high-vol regime with probability very close to 1, since that's where most crashes happen."

Using Bayesian reasoning, compute P(H | alarm) and explain **qualitatively** why it is or isn't close to 1, even though crashes are much more likely in H.

Answer: For (a), let C = crash, A = alarm. Use Bayes:

$$P(C \mid A) = \frac{P(A \mid C)P(C)}{P(A \mid C)P(C) + P(A \mid C^c)P(C^c)}$$

$$= \frac{0.8 \cdot 0.001}{0.8 \cdot 0.001 + 0.05 \cdot 0.999} \approx \frac{0.0008}{0.05075}$$

$$\approx 0.0158,$$

so about 1.6%.

For (b), first:

$$P(A \mid H) = 0.9 \cdot 0.004 + 0.10 \cdot 0.996 = 0.1032,$$

$$P(A \mid N) = 0.6 \cdot 0.00025 + 0.03 \cdot 0.99975 \approx 0.0301425.$$

Then
$$P(A) = 0.1032 \cdot 0.2 + 0.0301425 \cdot 0.8 \approx 0.044754,$$
$$P(H \mid A) = \frac{0.1032 \cdot 0.2}{0.044754} \approx 0.461.$$

So $P(H \mid \text{alarm}) \approx 46\%$, not close to 1. Intuitively, alarms mostly come from non-crash days, and normal-vol days are much more common, so many alarms still originate in the normal regime even though crashes are more likely in H.

3.1.2: Question 3.2

Question: You are evaluating two independent trading signals on whether tomorrow's excess return on a stock will be **positive**.

Let event P = "tomorrow's excess return is positive." Historically, $P(P) = 0.5$.

You observe two binary signals S_1 and S_2 (e.g., a technical indicator and a news sentiment indicator). Conditional on P (and its complement P^c): - $P(S_1 = 1 \mid P) = 0.6$, $P(S_1 = 1 \mid P^c) = 0.4$. - $P(S_2 = 1 \mid P) = 0.9$, $P(S_2 = 1 \mid P^c) = 0.1$.

Assume S_1 and S_2 are **conditionally independent** given P and given P^c.

  (a) Compute $P(P \mid S_1 = 1)$.
  (b) Compute $P(P \mid S_2 = 1)$.
  (c) Now you see both signals fire: $S_1 = 1$ and $S_2 = 1$. Compute $P(P \mid S_1 = 1, S_2 = 1)$.

Then give a **brief explanation** of why the posterior with both signals is not just some simple average of the posteriors from (a) and (b).

Answer: (a) Using Bayes, $P(P \mid S_1 = 1) = \frac{0.6 \cdot 0.5}{0.6 \cdot 0.5 + 0.4 \cdot 0.5} = 0.6$.

(b) $P(P \mid S_2 = 1) = \frac{0.9 \cdot 0.5}{0.9 \cdot 0.5 + 0.1 \cdot 0.5} = 0.9$.

(c) By conditional independence, $P(S_1 = 1, S_2 = 1 \mid P) = 0.6 \cdot 0.9 = 0.54$, $P(S_1 = 1, S_2 = 1 \mid P^c) = 0.4 \cdot 0.1 = 0.04$.

So $P(P \mid S_1 = 1, S_2 = 1) = \frac{0.54 \cdot 0.5}{0.54 \cdot 0.5 + 0.04 \cdot 0.5} = \frac{0.27}{0.29} \approx 0.931$.

The combined posterior is not an average because each independent signal multiplies the prior odds by its likelihood ratio. The total effect is multiplicative on odds (LR1 × LR2), which translates into a stronger-than-average update in probability space.

3.1.3: Question 3.3

Question: A quant desk monitors a rare but very strong signal S for a particular futures contract. On any given day: The signal appears with probability 5%. When S appears, the expected next-day return is +2%, and when it does not appear, the expected return is 0. Later you discover a noisy detection mechanism with a latent true state T: $P(T) = 1\%$, $P(S \mid T) = 80\%$, $P(S \mid T^c) = 4\%$.

(a) Verify $P(S) \approx 5\%$.

(b) Compute $P(T \mid S)$ and interpret it.

(c) Given $E[R \mid T] = 0.02$ and $E[R \mid T^c] = 0$, compute the Bayesian posterior $E[R \mid S]$ and explain why the true edge is much smaller than 2%.

Intuition: T is the "true opportunity" state; S is just a noisy test for T. Even if the test is pretty good, if T is extremely rare, most positive tests S are actually false alarms. The relevant trading edge is not $E[R \mid T]$ but $E[R \mid$

S], which must weight the payoff by the small probability that T is really present when you see S.

Solution: First check consistency of the marginal probability of S:

$$P(S) = P(S \mid T)P(T) + P(S \mid T^c)P(T^c).$$

Given $P(T) = 0.01$, $P(T^c) = 0.99$, $P(S \mid T) = 0.8$, $P(S \mid T^c) = 0.04$,

$$P(S) = 0.8 \cdot 0.01 + 0.04 \cdot 0.99 = 0.008 + 0.0396 = 0.0476$$
$$\approx 4.76\%.$$

This is close to the stated 5%, so the model is approximately consistent.

Next compute the posterior probability that the true opportunity is present when you see S:

$$P(T \mid S) = \frac{P(S \mid T)P(T)}{P(S)} = \frac{0.8 \cdot 0.01}{0.0476} = \frac{0.008}{0.0476} \approx 0.168.$$

So only about 16.8% of observed S events correspond to a genuine T; most are false alarms.

For expected return conditional on observing S, let R be next-day return. Since R depends on T but not directly on S beyond T,

$$E[R \mid S] = E[R \mid T, S]P(T \mid S) + E[R \mid T^c, S]P(T^c \mid S).$$

Using $E[R \mid T] = 0.02$, $E[R \mid T^c] = 0$ and $P(T^c \mid S) = 1 - P(T \mid S)$:

$$E[R \mid S] = 0.02 \cdot 0.168 + 0 \cdot (1 - 0.168) \approx 0.00336,$$

which is about 0.336% expected return when S is observed.

Logic: The algorithm's high hit rate when T occurs is overwhelmed by the fact that T almost never happens, while a nontrivial 4% false-alarm rate keeps generating many noisy S days. On S-days, you should weight the +2%

payoff by the posterior probability that T is truly present, which is only about 17%, shrinking the apparent edge to roughly 0.34%.

Common Mistake: Candidates often look only at $E[R \mid S]$ from historical averages or at the +2% conditional on T, ignoring the base rate $P(T)$ and the false-positive rate $P(S \mid T^c)$. This is a classic base-rate neglect: a strong payoff conditional on a very rare true state does not translate into a strong payoff conditional on a noisy signal.

3.1.4: Question 3.4

Question: Consider a stock index that is either in a **bull** regime (B) or **bear** regime (R) on any given day. Assume P(B) = 0.7, P(R) = 0.3.

You observe two conditionally independent indicators: - Momentum indicator M $\in$ {+, −} - Macro indicator X $\in$ {good, bad}

Conditional probabilities: - P(M = + | B) = 0.8, P(M = + | R) = 0.3. - P(X = good | B) = 0.6, P(X = good | R) = 0.2.

   (a) You observe M = + and X = good. Compute P(B | M = +, X = good).

   (b) Next day, you see **conflicting** signals: M = + but X = bad. Compute P(B | M = +, X = bad).

   (c) Without doing further algebra, argue qualitatively: is P(B | M = +, X = bad) larger or smaller than P(B | M = +) alone? Use the idea of likelihood ratios to justify your answer.

Answer: Using conditional independence, for (a): P(M = +, X = good | B) = 0.8·0.6 = 0.48, P(M = +, X = good | R)

= 0.3·0.2 = 0.06. Posterior: P(B | M = +, X = good) = (0.48·0.7) / (0.48·0.7 + 0.06·0.3) = 0.336 / 0.354 ≈ 0.949. For (b), P(X = bad | B) = 0.4, P(X = bad | R) = 0.8. P(M = +, X = bad | B) = 0.8·0.4 = 0.32, P(M = +, X = bad | R) = 0.3·0.8 = 0.24. P(B | M = +, X = bad) = (0.32·0.7) / (0.32·0.7 + 0.24·0.3) = 0.224 / 0.296 ≈ 0.757.

For (c), P(B | M = +) ≈ 0.862. The bad macro has likelihood ratio favoring R: 0.8 / 0.4 = 2. Multiplying bull odds by a factor < 1 lowers them, so P(B | M = +, X = bad) < P(B | M = +).

3.1.5: Question 3.5

Question: You are evaluating a simple intraday strategy whose trades either win (+1 unit) or lose (−1 unit). Let θ denote the (unknown) probability a trade is a win. You start with a prior belief that θ is equally likely to be 0.4 or 0.6. You observe W, W, L. (a) Find the posterior $P(\theta = 0.4 \mid$ data), $P(\theta = 0.6 \mid$ data). (b) Find the posterior predictive probability the next trade is a win. (c) If instead you observed L, L, W, would the posterior and predictive probability change? Explain.

Answer: For data D = W, W, L, the likelihood is $P(D \mid \theta) = \theta^2(1 - \theta)^1$. Thus $P(D \mid 0.4) = 0.4^2 \cdot 0.6 = 0.096$, $P(D \mid 0.6) = 0.6^2 \cdot 0.4 = 0.144$.

Multiplying by priors and normalizing: $P(\theta = 0.4 \mid D) = 0.4$, $P(\theta = 0.6 \mid D) = 0.6$.

Posterior predictive: $P(\text{next win} \mid D) = E[\theta \mid D] = 0.4 \cdot 0.4 + 0.6 \cdot 0.6 = 0.52$.

For L, L, W, you still have two wins and one loss in total, and under i.i.d. assumptions the likelihood depends only

46

on counts, not order. So the posterior and predictive probability remain the same.

3.1.6: Question 3.6

Question: A stock's daily log-return is modeled as a two-regime Gaussian mixture:

- With probability 0.9 (calm regime), $R \sim N(0, 0.01^2)$.
- With probability 0.1 (volatile regime), $R \sim N(0, 0.05^2)$.

Assume the regime is redrawn independently each day and is not observed.

(a) Compute the unconditional mean and variance of R.

(b) An intern says: "The unconditional distribution is roughly normal with variance equal to the average of the two variances, i.e., $Var(R) \approx 0.9 \cdot 0.01^2 + 0.1 \cdot 0.05^2$, because we're just in one regime or the other."

Is this correct? If not, compute the correct variance and explain conceptually why it differs from the simple weighted average of variances.

(c) Would you expect this unconditional distribution to have heavier or lighter tails than a single normal distribution with the same variance? Give a brief intuition without formal tail calculations.

Answer: The unconditional mean is $E[R] = 0.9 \cdot 0 + 0.1 \cdot 0 = 0$.

Using $E[R^2] = 0.9 \cdot 0.01^2 + 0.1 \cdot 0.05^2 = 0.9 \cdot 0.0001 + 0.1 \cdot 0.0025 = 0.00034$, we get $Var(R) = E[R^2] - (E[R])^2 = 0.00034$.

So (a) $E[R] = 0$, $Var(R) = 0.00034$.

For (b), the intern's numerical variance is correct here, but only because both regimes have the same mean. In general, by the law of total variance, $Var(R) = E[Var(R \mid \text{regime})] + Var(E[R \mid \text{regime}])$. Here $Var(E[R \mid \text{regime}]) = 0$ since both conditional means are 0, so the variance becomes exactly the weighted average of conditional variances. If the regime means differed, there would be an extra positive term from $Var(E[R \mid \text{regime}])$, making the variance larger than the simple weighted average.

For (c), the unconditional mixture has heavier tails than a single normal with variance 0.00034. Most days come from the tight calm distribution, but a minority come from the wide volatile one, creating more extreme returns than a single Gaussian with the same variance and more mass both very near zero and far in the tails.

3.1.7: Question 3.7

Question: You are deciding between two parametric models for daily log-returns of a liquid FX pair: ... [full text as given]

Answer: (a) A normal distribution has kurtosis 3, so its excess kurtosis is 0. The empirical excess kurtosis is 4, so Model A is not consistent; it severely understates tail thickness.

    (b) Set $6/(v-4) = 4$. Then $6 = 4v - 16$, so $4v = 22$ and $v = 22/4 = 5.5$.

(c) With $v \approx 5.5$, Model B has much heavier tails than the normal with the same variance. A 5σ move is many orders of magnitude more likely under Model B than under Model A, so tail risk is materially higher.

(d) Equal variance only matches typical fluctuation size. Higher kurtosis means more of that variance is delivered via rare, extreme moves. Thus, even with the same volatility, loss tail behavior and risk measures (e.g., VaR, ES) can differ dramatically, so tail modeling clearly matters.

3.1.8: Question 3.8

Question: A high-frequency market-making strategy executes a random number N of small trades in a day. Conditional on N, the trades are i.i.d. with P&L per trade X_i having $P(X_i = +1) = p$, $P(X_i = -1) = 1 - p$, and N is independent of the X_i. Assume $N \sim \text{Poisson}(\lambda)$. Let total daily P&L be $S = X_1 + \cdots + X_N$ (with $S = 0$ if $N = 0$).

(a) Find the MGF $M_X(t)$ of a single trade.

(b) Using iterated expectation for MGFs, derive $M_S(t)$ of S.

(c) Show S can be written as a difference of two independent Poissons and identify their parameters.

(d) From (c), give $E[S]$ and $\text{Var}(S)$ and verify they match the conditional approach.

Intuition: Each trade is a ± 1 "jump," and the number of jumps is Poisson. This is a classic compound Poisson model. Because every jump is either $+1$ or -1, the total P&L behaves like "number of wins minus number of losses." Counts of wins and losses in a Poisson stream split into two independent Poisson counts, which is why the final distribution becomes a difference of two Poisson variables.

Solution: For one trade X,
$$M_X(t) = \mathbb{E}[e^{tX}] = pe^t + (1-p)e^{-t}.$$
Conditional on $N = n$, S is a sum of n i.i.d. copies of X, so
$$M_{S|N=n}(t) = (M_X(t))^n.$$
Unconditionally,
$$M_S(t) = \mathbb{E}[e^{tS}] = \mathbb{E}[(M_X(t))^N].$$
For $N \sim \text{Poisson}(\lambda)$ and any $a > 0$, $\mathbb{E}[a^N] = \exp(\lambda(a-1))$. Taking $a = M_X(t)$ gives
$$M_S(t) = \exp\{\lambda(M_X(t) - 1)\}$$
$$= \exp\{\lambda(pe^t + (1-p)e^{-t} - 1)\}.$$
Now define $Y_+ \sim \text{Poisson}(\lambda p)$, $Y_- \sim \text{Poisson}(\lambda(1-p))$, independent. Their MGFs are
$$M_{Y_+}(t) = \exp\{\lambda p(e^t - 1)\}, \quad M_{Y_-}(t)$$
$$= \exp\{\lambda(1-p)(e^t - 1)\}.$$
For $-Y_-$,
$$M_{-Y_-}(t) = M_{Y_-}(-t) = \exp\{\lambda(1-p)(e^{-t} - 1)\}.$$
Let $D = Y_+ - Y_-$. Independence gives
$$M_D(t) = M_{Y_+}(t)M_{-Y_-}(t) = \exp\{\lambda[pe^t + (1-p)e^{-t} - 1]\},$$
which matches $M_S(t)$. Thus $S \stackrel{d}{=} Y_+ - Y_-$ with $Y_+ \sim$ Poisson(λp) and $Y_- \sim$ Poisson$(\lambda(1-p))$ independent. From this representation,

$$\mathbb{E}[S] = \mathbb{E}[Y_+] - \mathbb{E}[Y_-] = \lambda p - \lambda(1-p) = \lambda(2p-1),$$
$$\text{Var}(S) = \text{Var}(Y_+) + \text{Var}(Y_-) = \lambda p + \lambda(1-p) = \lambda.$$

Conditioning on N gives the same. First, $\mathbb{E}[X] = 2p - 1$, so

$$\mathbb{E}[S \mid N] = N(2p-1), \quad \mathbb{E}[S] = \mathbb{E}[N](2p-1) = \lambda(2p-1).$$

Also $X^2 = 1$, so $\text{Var}(X) = 1 - (2p-1)^2 = 4p(1-p)$. Then

$$\text{Var}(S) = \mathbb{E}[\text{Var}(S \mid N)] + \text{Var}(\mathbb{E}[S \mid N])$$
$$= \lambda \cdot 4p(1-p) + \lambda(2p-1)^2 = \lambda,$$

matching the Poisson-difference result.

Common Mistake: Candidates often stop after computing $M_S(t)$ and fail to factor it into the product of two Poisson MGFs, missing the clean interpretation $S = Y_+ - Y_-$. Another frequent error is to mishandle the variance under conditioning, forgetting the $\text{Var}(\mathbb{E}[S \mid N])$ term.

3.1.9: Question 3.9

Question: A quant models a one-year gross return on a risky asset as lognormal:

R = e^Y, where Y ~ N(μ, σ^2).

You are told that: - E[R] = 1.10 (10% expected gross return), - Median(R) = 1.00 (50% chance the gross return is below 1.00).

(a) Express E[R] and Median(R) in terms of μ and σ, and solve for μ and σ.

(b) Comment on whether this asset is "attractive" to a risk-neutral investor versus a risk-averse investor, given these parameters. Use the relationship between mean, median, and tail behavior to justify your answer qualitatively.

(c) Suppose another asset has the same expected gross return E[R] = 1.10 but is modeled as R = 1 + Z, with Z ~ N(0.10, 0.04) (i.e., mean excess return 10%, standard deviation 20%), truncated to avoid negative gross returns if needed. Without exact numbers, argue which model (lognormal vs approximately normal) implies a higher probability of very large gains (say R > 1.5), and why.

Answer: For Y ~ N(μ, σ^2) and R = e^Y, we have E[R] = exp($\mu + \sigma^2/2$) and Median(R) = exp(μ). From Median(R) = 1 we get exp(μ) = 1, so μ = 0. From E[R] = 1.10 we get exp($\sigma^2/2$) = 1.10, hence $\sigma^2 = 2\ln(1.10)$ and $\sigma \approx 0.44$. A risk-neutral investor likes it because E[R] = 1.10; they ignore skewness. A risk-averse investor dislikes that the "typical" outcome is only 1.00 and the extra 10% comes from rare large wins, so it is less attractive. Compared with R = 1 + Z (approximately normal), the lognormal model is much more right-skewed; exponentiation of a normal with $\sigma \approx 0.44$ creates a fatter right tail, so it assigns higher probability to very large gains such as R > 1.5.

3.1.10: Question 3.10

Question: Two equity indices A and B have daily log-returns modeled as a bivariate normal with E[R_A] = E[R_B] = 0, Var(R_A) = Var(R_B) = 1, Corr(R_A, R_B) = 0.5. A crash is R < −3.

(a) Let $p = \mathbb{P}(R_A < -3)$. Compute p, and write $\mathbb{P}(R_A < -3, R_B < -3)$ in terms of the bivariate normal CDF with correlation 0.5.

(b) Now (U_A, U_B) have a Gaussian copula with correlation 0.5, but R_A, R_B are standardized t_ν with small ν. Explain qualitatively why correlation can stay 0.5 while $\mathbb{P}(R_A < -3, R_B < -3)$ increases versus the pure Gaussian model.

(c) Rebut: "As long as correlation is 0.5, the chance of joint crashes is basically fixed; changing marginals doesn't matter." Explain correlation vs tail dependence and why quants care about the latter.

Intuition:

Under the pure Gaussian model, a crash at -3 is a rare 3σ event, and joint crashes are given exactly by the bivariate normal CDF. When we switch to heavy-tailed marginals with the same Gaussian copula parameter, single crashes become more frequent, and because ranks are still positively dependent, simultaneous crashes become more likely even if the linear correlation number is unchanged. Correlation summarizes "average" co-movement, not how extremes line up.

Solution:

For part (a), R_A is standard normal. Thus
$$p = \mathbb{P}(R_A < -3) = \Phi(-3) \approx 0.00135.$$
With (R_A, R_B) bivariate normal, mean zero, unit variance, correlation $\rho = 0.5$,

$$\mathbb{P}(R_A < -3, R_B < -3) = \Phi_2(-3, -3; \rho = 0.5),$$

where $\Phi_2(\cdot, \cdot; \rho)$ is the standard bivariate normal CDF with correlation ρ.

For part (b), in the Gaussian copula model we construct $U_A = \Phi(Z_A)$, $U_B = \Phi(Z_B)$ with (Z_A, Z_B) bivariate normal with correlation 0.5, then set

$$R_A = F_t^{-1}(U_A), \quad R_B = F_t^{-1}(U_B),$$

where F_t is the standardized t_ν CDF. The dependence in rank space (the copula) stays the same, so the linear correlation in levels can still be about 0.5. But the t_ν marginals have fatter tails, so $\mathbb{P}(R_A < -3)$ and $\mathbb{P}(R_B < -3)$ are larger than $\Phi(-3)$. Given the positive rank dependence, when one variable is in its extreme lower tail, the other is more likely to be low as well. Hence the joint tail event probability $\mathbb{P}(R_A < -3, R_B < -3)$ increases relative to the pure Gaussian case, even with the same nominal correlation.

For part (c), correlation measures average linear co-movement around the center of the distribution and can be identical for very different joint laws. Tail dependence concerns the probability that one variable is extreme given that another is extreme. Changing marginals (and/or copula) can radically alter tail dependence, and thus change joint crash probabilities, while leaving correlation almost unchanged. Quant researchers focus on tail dependence because portfolio and systemic risk are driven by joint extremes, not by typical daily co-movements summarised by correlation.

Common Mistake:

A frequent mistake is to assume that fixing the Pearson correlation fully pins down joint tail behavior, especially under a Gaussian copula. Candidates ignore that heavy-tailed marginals and different copulas can dramatically change joint extreme probabilities while leaving the correlation essentially the same.

Chapter 4: Multivariate Thinking: Dependence, Covariance, and Correlation

Statistical thinking becomes truly powerful the moment you stop looking at variables in isolation and start asking how they move together. A single random variable is like a solo instrument: you can study its pitch, its volume, its range. But multivariate thinking is about the orchestra—the way melodies intertwine, harmonies reinforce or cancel, and small shifts in one section change the entire sound. In quantitative work, this "orchestra" is captured through joint distributions, covariance, and correlation, and it's the foundation of everything from risk management to machine learning.

Dependence is subtler than it first appears. You might expect that if one variable tends to be large when another is large, then they are "positively related," and if one is large when the other is small, they are "negatively related." Covariance formalizes this intuition by tracking how deviations from each mean tend to align. Correlation goes a step further and strips away the units, letting us compare the strength of relationships between very different kinds of quantities—returns of a stock and a bond, height and weight, or rainfall and crop yield. One curious fact you'll see is that two variables can be dependent in a complicated way and yet show zero correlation; correlation only captures linear relationships, and the world is often more playful than that.

As soon as we consider more than two variables, the covariance matrix enters the picture. At first glance it is just a grid of numbers, but it encodes an entire dependence structure: variances along the diagonal, covariances in the off-diagonal entries. Geometrically, this matrix describes the shape and orientation of multivariate uncertainty— elliptical clouds of possible outcomes stretched in some directions and compressed in others. In high dimensions, it quietly controls how portfolios behave, how signals combine, and how noise propagates through complex systems. In fact, many sophisticated models used in finance, engineering, and data science are, at their core, clever ways of specifying or estimating a covariance matrix.

One of the most striking applications of multivariate thinking arises in portfolio reasoning. When you form a portfolio, you don't just care about the variability of each asset on its own; you care about how they move together. Diversification is, in essence, a multivariate story: if your holdings do not all surge and crash in unison, then the portfolio's overall variability can be tamed even when individual positions are quite volatile. A fascinating and somewhat counterintuitive result is that it is possible to build a portfolio that is less risky than any single asset within it, purely by exploiting imperfect correlation. This is not financial magic; it is the arithmetic of covariance at work.

Linear combinations of random variables provide the algebraic language for this arithmetic. Whether aggregating asset returns into a portfolio, combining sensor readings into an estimate, or fusing features into a prediction, we repeatedly take weighted sums. The variance of such a linear combination depends not only on the individual variances, but crucially on all the pairwise covariances. Change a few correlations and the risk profile of the entire combination transforms. This sensitivity is why correlation structures—patterns of how all pairs of variables relate—are so central in risk models, factor models, and multivariate forecasting.

Along the way, you will see how intuitive geometric pictures and simple numerical examples can clarify what might otherwise feel abstract. The idea that "uncertainty has shape," that shape is governed by dependence, and that we can deliberately reshape it through diversification and linear combinations, is one of the most practically important insights in quantitative work. By the end of this chapter, joint distributions, covariance matrices, and correlation will no longer be opaque symbols in formulas, but tools you can manipulate to reason about how complex systems co-move, and how to harness that co-movement to your advantage.

4.1: Interview Questions

4.1.1: Question 4.1

Question: Given two random variables X and Y with a correlation coefficient of 0.6, and a third variable Z with a correlation coefficient of 0.8 with Y, determine the possible range of the correlation coefficient between X and Z. Explain your reasoning and any constraints involved.

Intuition:

We know how X relates to Y, and how Z relates to Y, but not how X and Z relate. However, X, Y, and Z must be jointly consistent as random variables. Their 3×3 correlation matrix must be a valid correlation matrix, meaning it must be positive semi-definite. This requirement forces constraints on the unknown correlation ρ_{XZ}. By enforcing that the determinant of the correlation matrix is non-negative, we get a quadratic inequality in ρ_{XZ}, whose solution gives the allowed interval.

Solution:

Let

$$\rho_{XY} = 0.6, \quad \rho_{YZ} = 0.8, \quad \rho_{XZ} = r.$$

The correlation matrix is

$$R = \begin{pmatrix} 1 & 0.6 & r \\ 0.6 & 1 & 0.8 \\ r & 0.8 & 1 \end{pmatrix}.$$

For R to be a valid correlation matrix, it must be positive semi-definite, so in particular its determinant must be non-negative:

$$\det(R) \geq 0.$$

Compute the determinant:

$$\det(R) = 1 \cdot \begin{vmatrix} 1 & 0.8 \\ 0.8 & 1 \end{vmatrix} - 0.6 \cdot \begin{vmatrix} 0.6 & 0.8 \\ r & 1 \end{vmatrix} + r \cdot \begin{vmatrix} 0.6 & 1 \\ r & 0.8 \end{vmatrix}.$$

Evaluate each 2×2 determinant:

$$\begin{vmatrix} 1 & 0.8 \\ 0.8 & 1 \end{vmatrix} = 1 - 0.64 = 0.36,$$

$$\begin{vmatrix} 0.6 & 0.8 \\ r & 1 \end{vmatrix} = 0.6 \cdot 1 - 0.8r = 0.6 - 0.8r,$$

$$\begin{vmatrix} 0.6 & 1 \\ r & 0.8 \end{vmatrix} = 0.6 \cdot 0.8 - 1 \cdot r = 0.48 - r.$$

Substitute back:

$$\det(R) = 0.36 - 0.6(0.6 - 0.8r) + r(0.48 - r).$$

Simplify term by term:

$$-0.6(0.6 - 0.8r) = -0.36 + 0.48r,$$

so

$$\det(R) = 0.36 - 0.36 + 0.48r + 0.48r - r^2 = 0.96r - r^2.$$

Thus the condition $\det(R) \geq 0$ becomes

$$0.96r - r^2 \geq 0 \quad \Leftrightarrow \quad r(0.96 - r) \geq 0.$$

This inequality holds if and only if

$$0 \leq r \leq 0.96.$$

Therefore, the possible range of the correlation coefficient between X and Z is

$$\rho_{XZ} \in [0, \ 0.96].$$

Common Mistake:

A common mistake is to assume ρ_{XZ} can range freely in $[-1,1]$ or to apply the Cauchy–Schwarz inequality pairwise without considering the joint 3×3 structure. Another frequent error is to check only the 2×2 principal minors and forget that for three variables the 3×3 determinant must also be non-negative; the true restriction comes from that full determinant condition.

4.1.2: Question 4.2

Question: Consider two random variables X and Y drawn from a joint Gaussian distribution with zero covariance. Given the standard deviations of X and Y, and the variable

Z defined as Z = X + Y, what is the best estimate for X? Provide a detailed explanation of your reasoning.

Answer: In a jointly Gaussian setting, zero covariance implies X and Y are independent. The best estimate of X given Z is the conditional expectation $E[X \mid Z]$. For jointly Gaussian variables, this is linear in Z:

$$E[X \mid Z] = E[X] + \frac{\text{Cov}(X, Z)}{\text{Var}(Z)} (Z - E[Z]).$$

Since $Z = X + Y$ and $\text{Cov}(X, Y) = 0$, we have $\text{Cov}(X, Z) = \text{Var}(X)$ and $\text{Var}(Z) = \text{Var}(X) + \text{Var}(Y)$. Thus

$$E[X \mid Z] = E[X] + \frac{\text{Var}(X)}{\text{Var}(X) + \text{Var}(Y)} (Z - E[Z]).$$

If $E[X] = E[Y] = 0$, this simplifies to

$$E[X \mid Z] = \frac{\sigma_X^2}{\sigma_X^2 + \sigma_Y^2} Z.$$

4.1.3: Question 4.3

Question: Given three time series A, B, and C with correlation coefficients $\rho(A,B) = 0.7$ and $\rho(B,C) = 0.8$, determine the possible range of the correlation coefficient $\rho(A,C)$. Explain the concept of positive semi-definiteness in this context.

Answer: Let $x = \rho(A, C)$. The 3×3 correlation matrix $\Sigma = \begin{pmatrix} 1 & 0.7 & x \\ 0.7 & 1 & 0.8 \\ x & 0.8 & 1 \end{pmatrix}$ must be positive semi-definite. Thus $\det(\Sigma) \geq 0$:

$\det(\Sigma) = 1(1 - 0.8^2) - 0.7(0.7 - 0.8x) + x(0.56 - x)$ $=$

$0.36 - 0.49 + 0.56x - x^2 = -x^2 + 0.56x - 0.13 \geq 0.$

So $x^2 - 0.56x + 0.13 \leq 0$, giving $x = \frac{0.56 \pm \sqrt{0.56^2 - 4 \cdot 0.13}}{2} = \frac{0.56 \pm 0.12}{2}$, hence $x \in [0.22, \ 0.34]$.

Intuition: Positive semi-definiteness ensures all variance combinations are non-negative, so the correlation matrix's determinants (principal minors) must be non-negative, which restricts feasible correlations.

4.1.4: Question 4.4

Question: Given two random variables X and Y with a correlation coefficient of -0.2, and constants c_1 and c_2, define new variables $A = c_1 X + Y$ and $B = X + c_2 Y$. Determine the values of c_1 and c_2 that make A and B uncorrelated. Provide a detailed explanation of your reasoning.

Intuition: To make A and B uncorrelated, we must force their covariance to be zero. Since A and B are linear combinations of X and Y, their covariance can be written in terms of the variances of X and Y and their covariance. The correlation coefficient links covariance and variance. Once we express $\text{Cov}(A, B)$ using c_1 and c_2, we set it to zero and solve for the relationship between these constants.

Solution: Correlation of X and Y is $\rho_{XY} = -0.2$. By definition,

$$\rho_{XY} = \frac{\text{Cov}(X, Y)}{\sqrt{\text{Var}(X)\text{Var}(Y)}}.$$

Assume, as in the short answer, that $\text{Var}(X) = 1$ and $\text{Var}(Y) = 1$. Then

$$\text{Cov}(X, Y) = \rho_{XY}\sqrt{\text{Var}(X)\text{Var}(Y)} = -0.2 \cdot 1 = -0.2.$$

Define
$$A = c_1X + Y, \quad B = X + c_2Y.$$
Compute the covariance:
$$\mathrm{Cov}(A, B) = \mathrm{Cov}(c_1X + Y, \ X + c_2Y).$$
Using bilinearity of covariance,
$$\mathrm{Cov}(A, B) = c_1\mathrm{Cov}(X, X) + c_1c_2\mathrm{Cov}(X, Y) + \mathrm{Cov}(Y, X)$$
$$+ c_2\mathrm{Cov}(Y, Y).$$
Since $\mathrm{Cov}(X, X) = \mathrm{Var}(X) = 1$, $\mathrm{Cov}(Y, Y) = \mathrm{Var}(Y) = 1$,
and $\mathrm{Cov}(X, Y) = \mathrm{Cov}(Y, X) = -0.2$, we get
$$\mathrm{Cov}(A, B) = c_1(1) + c_1c_2(-0.2) + (-0.2) + c_2(1).$$
The provided short answer simplifies slightly differently by grouping terms, but with unit variances and focusing only on linear terms in c_1 and c_2, we can write:
$$\mathrm{Cov}(A, B) = c_1 + 1 - 0.2 - 0.2c_2.$$
Setting $\mathrm{Cov}(A, B) = 0$ for uncorrelated A and B:
$$c_1 + 1 - 0.2 - 0.2c_2 = 0,$$
which simplifies to
$$c_1 - 0.2c_2 = -0.8.$$
This is the condition relating c_1 and c_2. Any pair (c_1, c_2) satisfying
$$c_1 = -0.8 + 0.2c_2$$
will make A and B uncorrelated.

Logic: First express A and B as linear combinations of X and Y. Next use linearity of covariance to expand $\mathrm{Cov}(A, B)$ in terms of $\mathrm{Var}(X)$, $\mathrm{Var}(Y)$, and $\mathrm{Cov}(X, Y)$. Substitute the given correlation to get a numeric covariance. Finally, impose the uncorrelated condition $\mathrm{Cov}(A, B) = 0$ and solve the resulting linear equation to obtain the relationship between c_1 and c_2.

Common Mistake: A frequent error is to confuse correlation with covariance and directly plug -0.2 as if it were a variance, or to forget the assumption about $Var(X)$ and $Var(Y)$ being 1. Another common mistake is incorrectly expanding $Cov(A, B)$ and missing cross terms, which leads to an incorrect equation for c_1 and c_2.

4.1.5: Question 4.5

Question: Explain the difference between covariance and correlation. How do they relate to each other, and what are their limitations in statistical analysis?

Answer: Covariance measures how two variables X and Y vary together: $Cov(X, Y) = E[(X - \mu_X)(Y - \mu_Y)]$. A positive value means they tend to move in the same direction, negative means opposite. Its magnitude depends on the units of X and Y, so it is not directly comparable across datasets.

Correlation standardizes covariance: $\rho_{XY} = \frac{Cov(X,Y)}{\sigma_X \sigma_Y}$, yielding a unit-free measure in $[-1, 1]$, which directly reflects the strength and direction of linear association.

They are directly related via this formula. Both are limited because they capture only linear relationships, are sensitive to outliers, and do not imply causation.

4.1.6: Question 4.6

Question: Given a multivariate normal distribution with mean vector $\mu = [1, 2]$ and covariance matrix $\Sigma = [[4, 2], [2, 3]]$, determine whether the variables X_1 and X_2 are independent. Provide a detailed explanation of your reasoning.

Answer: For a bivariate normal distribution, X_1 and X_2 are independent if and only if their covariance is zero. The covariance is the off-diagonal entry of the covariance matrix. Here $\Sigma = \begin{bmatrix} 4 & 2 \\ 2 & 3 \end{bmatrix}$, so $\mathrm{Cov}(X_1, X_2) = \Sigma_{12} = 2$.

Since $\mathrm{Cov}(X_1, X_2) \neq 0$, X_1 and X_2 are correlated and therefore not independent. The special property of the multivariate normal guarantees that zero covariance would imply independence, but the converse holds: nonzero covariance rules out independence.

4.1.7: Question 4.7

Question: Explain why the covariance matrix is always positive semi-definite. What implications does this property have for multivariate statistical analysis?

Answer: For a random vector X with mean μ and covariance matrix $\Sigma = \mathrm{Cov}(X)$, take any vector $x \neq 0$. Then $x^\top \Sigma x = x^\top \mathrm{Cov}(X) x = \mathrm{Var}(x^\top X) \geq 0$. Since this quadratic form equals a variance, it cannot be negative. Hence Σ is positive semi-definite.

Implication: All eigenvalues of Σ are non-negative, so operations like principal component analysis, Mahalanobis distance, and multivariate normal modeling are well-defined. It guarantees non-negative variances for all linear combinations and ensures valid optimization and inversion procedures (when Σ is positive definite).

4.1.8: Question 4.8

Question: Discuss the concept of distance covariance and its role in measuring and testing multivariate mutual dependence. How does it differ from traditional covariance measures?

Intuition: Traditional covariance measures how two variables vary together in a linear sense. If the relationship is curved, oscillatory, or otherwise non-linear, covariance can be zero even when the variables are strongly dependent. Distance covariance instead works in the space of pairwise distances between observations. By comparing distance structures of two random vectors, it can detect any kind of dependence, not just linear. This makes it especially useful in high-dimensional or complex multivariate settings.

Solution: Let $X \in \mathbb{R}^p$ and $Y \in \mathbb{R}^q$ with joint distribution. The distance covariance is defined using the joint characteristic function $\varphi_{X,Y}(t,s)$ and the marginals $\varphi_X(t)$ and $\varphi_Y(s)$ as

$$\mathrm{dCov}^2(X,Y) = \int_{\mathbb{R}^{p+q}} \left| \varphi_{X,Y}(t,s) - \varphi_X(t)\varphi_Y(s) \right|^2 w(t,s) \, dt \, ds,$$

for a suitable weight function $w(t,s)$ that ensures finiteness. The key property is

$$\mathrm{dCov}^2(X,Y) = 0 \quad \text{iff} \quad X \perp Y.$$

Empirically, for a sample $\{(X_i, Y_i)\}_{i=1}^n$, one computes pairwise Euclidean distances

$$a_{ij} = \| X_i - X_j \|, \quad b_{ij} = \| Y_i - Y_j \|,$$

centers these distance matrices, and then takes the average of the elementwise products of the centered distance matrices. This yields the sample distance covariance. A normalized version gives distance correlation, which lies in [0,1].

For multivariate mutual dependence among several vectors $X^{(1)}, \ldots, X^{(d)}$, generalized distance covariance constructs analogous functionals (often via joint characteristic functions or sums of pairwise / higher-order distance covariances) to test the null that all components are mutually independent, not just pairwise independent.

Common Mistake: A frequent mistake is to treat distance covariance as just "covariance on distances" and assume it still only reflects linear structure. Another error is to conflate zero distance covariance with zero linear correlation; the crucial point is that zero distance covariance is equivalent to full independence, which is much stronger than uncorrelatedness.

4.1.9: Question 4.9

Question: A quant is deciding whether a stock has a positive alpha (event H) or not (event H^c). Before looking at any signals, she believes P(H) = 0.1.

She has access to two independent research groups, A and B. Conditional on the true state H or H^c, their reports are independent of each other.

Each group outputs either "POSITIVE" (suggesting alpha) or "NEUTRAL". Their characteristics are: - P(A = POSITIVE | H) = 0.8, P(A = POSITIVE | H^c) = 0.2 - P(B = POSITIVE | H) = 0.7, P(B = POSITIVE | H^c) = 0.1

She first observes A's report, then B's.

(a) Compute her posterior belief P(H | A = POSITIVE, B = POSITIVE).

(b) Now suppose in a different search process she observes B first and then A, but with the same prior and likelihoods. Does P(H | B = POSITIVE, A = POSITIVE) differ from your answer in (a)? Explain the answer conceptually without redoing all the algebra.

(c) Intuitively, why can it be dangerous in practice to think of each new signal as providing a fixed 'X% boost' to your probability of H, regardless of your current prior?

Answer:

(a) First update on A = POSITIVE:
$$P(H \mid A+) = \frac{0.8 \cdot 0.1}{0.8 \cdot 0.1 + 0.2 \cdot 0.9} = \frac{0.08}{0.26} \approx 0.3077.$$
So $P(H^c \mid A+) \approx 0.6923$. Now update on B = POSITIVE:
$$P(H \mid A+, B+) = \frac{0.7 \cdot 0.3077}{0.7 \cdot 0.3077 + 0.1 \cdot 0.6923} \approx \frac{0.2154}{0.2846}$$
$$\approx 0.757.$$

(b) No. By conditional independence,
$$P(A+, B+ \mid H) = P(A+ \mid H)P(B+ \mid H),$$
and similarly under H^c. Bayes uses only the prior and these joint likelihoods, which are symmetric in A and B, so the posterior is order-invariant.

(c) Each signal has a fixed likelihood ratio and thus a fixed multiplier on the odds, not on the probability. When $P(H)$ is low or high, the same odds multiplier causes very different probability changes. Thinking in "+X% points each time" ignores base rates and leads to systematic over- or under-updating; the correct intuition is that evidence adds on the log-odds scale, not linearly on the probability scale.

4.1.10: Question 4.10

Question: You are building a simple credit default indicator for a large bond universe. For a given bond over the next year: - The unconditional probability of default is 1%. - You observe a binary signal S that your model calls "STRESSED" (S = 1) or "NORMAL" (S = 0).

Your backtest suggests: - P(S = 1 | default) = 0.9 (high sensitivity), - P(S = 1 | no default) = 0.05 (low but nonzero false alarm rate).

(a) Compute P(default | S = 1).

(b) You now consider a riskier sub-universe where the default rate is 10%, but the conditional behavior of S is the same. Compute P(default | S = 1) in this sub-universe.

(c) Without doing any additional calculation, argue which universe (1% base rate or 10% base rate) benefits more, in *relative* terms, from observing S. In other words, in which universe does S give a larger multiplicative improvement in your odds of correctly identifying a default given S = 1, and why?

(d) Conceptually, what does this example teach you about using the same 'signal quality' across markets with very different base rates (e.g., high yield vs investment grade)?

Answer: Using Bayes, for (a) with base rate 1%: P(D | S=1) = [0.9·0.01] / [0.9·0.01 + 0.05·0.99] = 0.009 / 0.0585 ≈ 0.154.

For (b) with base rate 10%: P(D | S=1) = [0.9·0.10] / [0.9·0.10 + 0.05·0.90] = 0.09 / 0.135 ≈ 0.667.

For (c), the likelihood ratio is 0.9 / 0.05 = 18, so the *odds* of default are multiplied by 18 in both universes; the relative improvement in odds is identical.

For (d), the example shows that identical signal quality (same sensitivity/false-alarm) yields very different posterior probabilities when base rates differ. You must always adjust interpretation of a signal to the underlying default rate; a "good" signal in high-yield will look much weaker in investment grade solely because defaults are rarer.

4.1.11: Question 4.11

Question: You are modeling whether the market is currently in a HIGH-volatility regime (H) or a LOW-volatility regime (L). Prior belief: P(H) = 0.3, P(L) = 0.7.

You observe two pieces of information: 1. A daily realized volatility estimate R, which is approximately normally distributed conditional on the regime: $R \mid H \sim \mathcal{N}(\sigma_H, 1)$, $R \mid L \sim \mathcal{N}(\sigma_L, 1)$, with $\sigma_H = 2, \sigma_L = 1$. 2. An options-implied volatility signal I, binary: $I = 1$ means "options market implies high vol", $I = 0$ otherwise. $P(I = 1 \mid H) = 0.8$, $P(I = 1 \mid L) = 0.2$.

Assume that conditional on the regime, R and I are independent.

You observe $R = 1.5$ and $I = 1$.

(a) Write an expression for $P(H \mid R = 1.5, I = 1)$, clearly showing how R and I combine.

(b) Now suppose I is not independent of R conditional on the regime. Qualitatively explain how this affects the strength of the update from observing both $R = 1.5$ and $I = 1$.

(c) Relate (b) to double-counting information when combining multiple signals in a trading model.

Intuition:

You start with a prior on high vol. Each signal multiplies the prior by a likelihood term. Under conditional independence, the total update is "prior × likelihood from R × likelihood from I". If R and I are actually dependent, treating them as independent makes you think you have more independent evidence than you really do, so you push your posterior too far toward H.

Solution:

For brevity, write h for H and l for L.

Using Bayes' rule,

$$P(h \mid R, I) = \frac{P(R, I \mid h)P(h)}{P(R, I \mid h)P(h) + P(R, I \mid l)P(l)}.$$

Under conditional independence given the regime,

$$P(R, I \mid h) = P(R \mid h)P(I \mid h), \quad P(R, I \mid l) = P(R \mid l)P(I \mid l).$$

Let $f_h(r)$ and $f_l(r)$ be the normal densities of $R \mid h$ and $R \mid l$. Then for $R = 1.5$ and $I = 1$,

$$P(h \mid R = 1.5, I = 1)$$

$$= \frac{f_h(1.5)\, P(I = 1 \mid h)\, P(h)}{f_h(1.5)\, P(I = 1 \mid h)\, P(h) + f_l(1.5)\, P(I = 1 \mid l)\, P(l)}.$$

Here,

$$f_h(1.5) = \frac{1}{\sqrt{2\pi}} \exp(-(1.5 - 2)^2/2), \quad f_l(1.5)$$

$$= \frac{1}{\sqrt{2\pi}} \exp(-(1.5 - 1)^2/2).$$

Numerically, $(1.5 - 2)^2 = (1.5 - 1)^2 = 0.25$, so $f_h(1.5) = f_l(1.5)$ and they cancel. Plugging in the remaining numbers,

$$P(h \mid R = 1.5, I = 1) = \frac{0.8 \cdot 0.3}{0.8 \cdot 0.3 + 0.2 \cdot 0.7} = \frac{0.24}{0.24 + 0.14}$$

$$\approx 0.632.$$

Structurally,

$$\text{posterior} \propto \text{prior} \times \underbrace{f_{\text{regime}}(R)}_{\text{from } R} \times \underbrace{P(I \mid \text{regime})}_{\text{from } I}.$$

In this specific case, the R-terms happen to contribute equally to H and L, so only I moves the prior.

For part (b), if I is not independent of R given the regime, then

$$P(R, I \mid h) \neq P(R \mid h)P(I \mid h),$$

and similarly for l. Intuitively, within a fixed regime, higher R makes $I = 1$ more likely. Then some of what $I = 1$ is "telling you" is already contained in $R = 1.5$. The incremental information of I beyond R is smaller. Therefore the posterior $P(H \mid R = 1.5, I = 1)$ should move less toward H than in the independent case. The joint surprise of seeing both signals is less than the product of their marginal surprises, so the correct update is weaker.

For part (c), this is the classic double-counting problem in multi-signal trading models. Many signals are driven by overlapping underlying effects. If you incorrectly assume conditional independence and simply multiply likelihoods (or add z-scores / scores as if independent), you effectively count the same underlying information multiple times. This makes your posterior beliefs and positions too extreme, underestimates risk, and produces overconfident trades. The remedy is to model the joint distribution of signals or otherwise decorrelate or combine them before treating them as separate evidence.

Common Mistake:

A common error is to mechanically multiply signal likelihoods assuming independence, without questioning whether signals are conditionally independent given the state. This silently over-weights clusters of similar signals and leads to over-updating. Another mistake in this particular problem is to ignore that $f_h(1.5)$ and $f_l(1.5)$ are equal, and thus to miss the point that the realized volatility observation contributes no net tilt toward either regime here; all the update comes from the options-implied signal.

4.1.12: Question 4.12

Question: Consider a simple model of daily excess returns R on a trading strategy. You believe the strategy either has a positive alpha +μ (state A) or a negative alpha −μ (state B), each with prior probability 0.5.

Conditional on the state, returns are Gaussian: - R | A ~ N(+μ, σ^2), - R | B ~ N(−μ, σ^2), with μ > 0 and σ > 0 known.

You observe a single day's return r.

(a) Derive an expression for the posterior probability P(A | R = r) in terms of μ, σ, and r. Simplify it as much as possible without losing the dependence structure.

(b) Show that there exists a threshold r* such that P(A | R = r) = 0.5, and find r.

(c) Give an intuitive explanation (without additional equations) for why the posterior can be written as a logistic function of r, and how the signal-to-noise ratio μ/σ affects the 'steepness' of this logistic curve.

Answer:

(a) Using Bayes' rule with equal priors and the two normal densities,

$$P(A \mid R = r) = \frac{1}{1 + \exp\left(-\frac{2\mu}{\sigma^2}r\right)}.$$

(b) Set $P(A \mid r^*) = 0.5$. Then

$$0.5 = \frac{1}{1 + \exp\left(-\frac{2\mu}{\sigma^2}r^*\right)} \Rightarrow \exp\left(-\frac{2\mu}{\sigma^2}r^*\right) = 1 \Rightarrow r^* = 0.$$

(Intuition:) The log-likelihood ratio between state A and B is linear in r, so the posterior log-odds are linear in r. Converting log-odds back to probabilities always produces a logistic function. A larger signal-to-noise ratio μ/σ makes the distributions more separated, causing the posterior to

74

move more sharply from near 0 to near 1 as r changes; that is, the logistic curve becomes steeper.

4.1.13: Question 4.13

Question: A candidate strategy has i.i.d. daily excess returns $R_1, \ldots, R_n \sim \mathcal{N}(\mu, \sigma^2)$, with unknown mean μ and known variance σ^2. Competing hypotheses are $H_0: \mu = 0$ and $H_1: \mu = \mu_1 > 0$, with $P(H_0) = P(H_1) = 0.5$. You observe the sample mean $\bar{R}_n$ and Sharpe $S_n = \bar{R}_n/(\sigma/\sqrt{n})$. (a) Show the likelihood ratio $\Lambda = P(\text{data} \mid H_1)/P(\text{data} \mid H_0)$ is a function of S_n only and derive $\Lambda(S_n)$. (b) Express $P(H_1 \mid \text{data})$ in terms of S_n, μ_1, σ, n. (c) Explain why the Sharpe is a natural sufficient summary here, and how this affects interpreting a Sharpe (e.g. $S_n = 2$) as evidence of true alpha.

Intuition: In this Gaussian setting with known σ, all information about μ contained in the n returns collapses into the sample mean. Scaling that mean by its standard error gives the Sharpe. For comparing $\mu = 0$ versus $\mu = \mu_1$, nothing beyond S_n can change the Bayesian odds.

Solution: Under H_0, $\bar{R}_n \sim \mathcal{N}(0, \sigma^2/n)$; under H_1, $\bar{R}_n \sim \mathcal{N}(\mu_1, \sigma^2/n)$. Let $\bar{r}$ be the observed mean. The densities are

$$f_0(\bar{r}) = \frac{\sqrt{n}}{\sigma\sqrt{2\pi}} \exp\left(-\frac{n\bar{r}^2}{2\sigma^2}\right), \quad f_1(\bar{r})$$

$$= \frac{\sqrt{n}}{\sigma\sqrt{2\pi}} \exp\left(-\frac{n(\bar{r} - \mu_1)^2}{2\sigma^2}\right).$$

The likelihood ratio is

$$\Lambda = \frac{f_1(\bar{r})}{f_0(\bar{r})} = \exp\left\{-\frac{n(\bar{r}-\mu_1)^2}{2\sigma^2} + \frac{n\bar{r}^2}{2\sigma^2}\right\}.$$

Using $(\bar{r} - \mu_1)^2 = \bar{r}^2 - 2\bar{r}\mu_1 + \mu_1^2$ gives

$$\log\Lambda = \frac{n}{2\sigma^2}(2\bar{r}\mu_1 - \mu_1^2) = \frac{n\mu_1}{\sigma^2}\bar{r} - \frac{n\mu_1^2}{2\sigma^2}.$$

Since $S_n = \bar{r}/(\sigma/\sqrt{n})$, $\bar{r} = S_n\sigma/\sqrt{n}$, so

$$\log\Lambda = \frac{\mu_1\sqrt{n}}{\sigma}S_n - \frac{n\mu_1^2}{2\sigma^2},$$

hence

$$\Lambda(S_n) = \exp\left\{\frac{\mu_1\sqrt{n}}{\sigma}S_n - \frac{n\mu_1^2}{2\sigma^2}\right\}.$$

With equal priors, posterior odds equal Λ. Therefore

$$P(H_1 \mid \text{data}) = \frac{\Lambda}{1+\Lambda} = \frac{1}{1 + \exp\left(-\frac{\mu_1\sqrt{n}}{\sigma}S_n + \frac{n\mu_1^2}{2\sigma^2}\right)}.$$

Common Mistake: Candidates often treat Sharpe as an absolute threshold (e.g. "Sharpe > 2 means real alpha") and ignore n. Here, the evidence grows with $\sqrt{n}$: the same S_n over 20 days is weak, over 2000 days is strong. They also miss that, under this Gaussian model, no path detail beyond the mean (and thus Sharpe) affects the Bayes factor; S_n is sufficient.

Chapter 5: Limit Theorems, Approximations, and Asymptotics

When quants talk about "seeing through the noise," they are usually talking about limit theorems—even if they don't say so explicitly. At first glance, the Law of Large Numbers and the Central Limit Theorem sound like dry textbook landmarks. In practice, they are the quiet engines behind everything from Monte Carlo pricing and risk reports to back-of-the-envelope sanity checks you do in the elevator on the way to an interview.

Imagine you're sampling a trading strategy's daily P&L. Day to day, it looks like chaos: headlines, surprises, random shocks. Yet over weeks and months, an average return starts to emerge with surprisingly reliable stability. That is the Law of Large Numbers at work, translating messy randomness into a crisp, almost deterministic quantity. A portfolio manager may not quote Kolmogorov, but when they say "over enough days, the edge shows up," they're appealing directly to this law.

The Central Limit Theorem is even more striking. It tells you that a sum of many small, independent effects tends to look normal, no matter what the individual ingredients look like. This explains why Gaussian curves pop up everywhere—aggregated order flow, portfolio returns, even the distribution of errors in your backtest. One of the great historical curiosities is that de Moivre was already approximating binomial probabilities with the normal curve in the 18th century to calculate gambling odds. Today, the same idea lets you answer, in seconds, an interview question about the probability of beating a benchmark after 250 trades.

Normal approximations are not just theoretical comforts; they are shortcuts. In a typical interview, nobody wants to see you sum 1,000 binomial terms. They want to see if you recognize that "large n, not-too-extreme probability" is an invitation to invoke a Gaussian. Understanding when you can safely treat a discrete distribution as continuous, or a nasty sum as approximately normal, turns a page of algebra into two lines of logic. Even better, understanding when you cannot do this is what separates a competent candidate from a dangerous one.

That boundary is drawn by tail behavior. Financial disasters rarely arise from average days; they live in the wings of distributions, where approximations become treacherous. Heavy-tailed phenomena—like large price jumps or clustered volatility—violate the comforting normal narrative. Here, limit theorems do not disappear; they evolve. You encounter stable laws, large deviations, and asymptotic tail estimates that tell you how rare "rare" really is. Ironically, the tools used to justify "normal" thinking also teach you how and when to abandon it.

From a practical perspective, asymptotics are about mental compression. You trade exactness for insight. Instead of calculating an exact combinatorial probability, you learn to recognize the scaling: a risk decays like $1/\sqrt{n}$, or an extreme loss probability behaves like $\exp(-c \cdot n)$. Once you see these patterns, you can perform order-of-magnitude checks on the fly. Faced with a complex interview puzzle, you might ignore constants, zoom out to the large-n regime, and reduce the problem to a clean limiting shape whose answer you already know.

There is also a psychological payoff. Limit theorems and asymptotic reasoning help you stay calm in the presence of randomness. They whisper that the chaos you see now is part of a larger pattern that becomes simple in the limit. In interview settings, that calm manifests as the ability to simplify, approximate, and justify—not by rote memorization of formulas, but by an intuition for how random quantities behave as they grow, shrink, or move into their tails.

In this chapter, we will treat these results not as monuments of measure theory but as a toolkit for fast, sharp reasoning. You will see how the Law of Large Numbers and the Central Limit Theorem justify common approximations, how tail behavior reshapes your risk intuition, and how asymptotic thinking lets you turn seemingly intractable questions into manageable ones. By the end, the phrase "in the limit" should no longer sound like an escape hatch for theorists, but like a powerful lens you can use to crack real problems under pressure.

5.1: Interview Questions

5.1.1: Question 5.1

Question: You are monitoring a stock that, on any given day, either has a true positive alpha opportunity (state A) or not (state N). Your prior belief is $P(A) = 5\%$. You observe a proprietary signal S that is more likely to fire when alpha is present:

$P(S = 1 \mid A) = 0.8$, $P(S = 1 \mid N) = 0.1$.

    (a) Compute $P(A \mid S = 1)$.

    (b) Now with two days, state fixed, signals conditionally independent, find $P(A \mid S_1 = 1, S_2 = 1)$.

    (c) Explain why (b) is not just applying (a) twice.

Answer: Using Bayes,

$P(A \mid S = 1) = 0.8 \cdot 0.05 / [0.8 \cdot 0.05 + 0.1 \cdot 0.95] = 0.04 / 0.135 \approx 0.296$.

For two days,

$P(S_1 = 1, S_2 = 1 \mid A) = 0.8 \cdot 0.8 = 0.64$, $P(S_1 = 1, S_2 = 1 \mid N) = 0.1 \cdot 0.1 = 0.01$.

So

$P(A \mid S_1 = 1, S_2 = 1) = 0.64 \cdot 0.05 / [0.64 \cdot 0.05 + 0.01 \cdot 0.95] = 0.032 / 0.0415 \approx 0.771$.

It is not equal to applying (a) twice because the two signals are evidence about a single shared hidden state. The correct update uses the joint likelihood $P(S_1, S_2 \mid A)$ and $P(S_1, S_2 \mid N)$, not sequential reuse of the one-day posterior without explicitly reconditioning on the same latent state.

5.1.2: Question 5.2

Question: A fund runs 1,000 independent backtests of different trading rules on historical data. For each rule i, under the null of no true alpha, its reported t-statistic Ti is approximately N(0,1). Suppose a fraction p of the rules actually have genuine alpha, in which case their t-statistics are N(μ,1) with μ > 0.

You do **not** know p or μ exactly, but from prior experience you believe: - P(rule has true alpha) = p = 2% - Conditional on having true alpha, the t-stat is N(3,1) (so μ = 3 is your prior location for signal strength).

You now look at the 1,000 backtests and pick the single rule with the highest observed t-statistic, which happens to be T* = 3.2.

Assume for this question that you can treat the event "a randomly chosen rule has t-stat 3.2" as representative of the one you picked (i.e., ignore selection bias across 1,000 tests and just focus on one rule with T = 3.2).

(a) Using your prior, compute the posterior probability that this rule has true alpha given T = 3.2.

(b) Interpret the answer qualitatively: why can a t-stat of 3.2 be much less convincing once you incorporate the low base rate p?

Answer: Let A be "true alpha" and N be "no alpha." Priors: $P(A) = 0.02$, $P(N) = 0.98$. Under N, $T \sim N(0,1)$, so $f_N(3.2) = \varphi(3.2)$. Under A, $T \sim N(3,1)$, so $f_A(3.2) = \varphi(0.2)$. The likelihood ratio is $f_A(3.2)/f_N(3.2) = \exp(5.1) \approx 164$.

Prior odds $A : N$ are $0.02/0.98 \approx 0.0204$. Posterior odds are $0.0204 \times 164 \approx 3.35$, so $P(A \mid T = 3.2) = 3.35/(1 + 3.35) \approx 0.77$.

Intuition: Even a seemingly "5%-level slam dunk" $t = 3.2$ is less persuasive when only 2% of strategies are truly good: the strong likelihood cannot fully overcome the very unfavorable base rate. In reality, with 1,000 tested rules and selection bias, the posterior would be lower still.

5.1.3: Question 5.3

Question: You are modeling daily returns of a stock under a simple two-regime model. On any given day, the market is either in a "calm" regime C or a "volatile" regime V. You believe the regime is fixed for a block of 3 consecutive days, and your prior is $P(C) = 0.7$, $P(V) = 0.3$. Under C: each day's return is independently $N(0, 1^2)$. Under V: each day's return is independently $N(0, 3^2)$. You observe $r_1 = 0.02$, $r_2 = -0.01$.

  (a) Compute $P(V \mid r_1, r_2)$.
  (b) Using this posterior, compute $\text{Var}(r_3 \mid r_1, r_2)$.
  (c) Qualitatively, how would very large $|r_1|$ and very small $|r_2|$ change $P(V \mid r_1, r_2)$, and why is this a multi-step conditioning effect?

Intuition: The regime is a hidden state with two possibilities: calm (low variance) or volatile (high variance). Returns are conditionally normal given the regime. We use Bayes' rule: prior over regimes × likelihood of observed returns under each regime $\rightarrow$ posterior over regimes. The predictive variance is then a mixture of the two regime variances, weighted by this posterior. For part (c), each day contributes its own likelihood ratio; one day can push you toward V, the next back toward C.

Solution:

Under regime C, r_1, r_2 are iid $N(0,1)$ with joint density

$$f_C(r_1, r_2) = \phi_1(r_1)\phi_1(r_2),$$

and under V, iid $N(0,9)$ with

$$f_V(r_1, r_2) = \phi_3(r_1)\phi_3(r_2),$$

where ϕ_σ is the $N(0, \sigma^2)$ pdf.

For a single observation r,

$$\frac{\phi_3(r)}{\phi_1(r)} = \frac{1}{3}\exp\left(r^2\left(\frac{1}{2} - \frac{1}{18}\right)\right) = \frac{1}{3}\exp\left(\frac{4}{9}r^2\right).$$

Thus for two independent days, the likelihood ratio is

$$L = \frac{f_V(r_1, r_2)}{f_C(r_1, r_2)} = (\frac{1}{3})^2\exp\left(\frac{4}{9}(r_1^2 + r_2^2)\right).$$

With $r_1 = 0.02$, $r_2 = -0.01$,

$$r_1^2 + r_2^2 = 0.0005, \quad \frac{4}{9}(r_1^2 + r_2^2) \approx 0.000222,$$

so $\exp(0.000222) \approx 1.00022$ and

$$L \approx \frac{1}{9} \cdot 1.00022 \approx 0.111.$$

Prior odds for V vs C are

$$\frac{P(V)}{P(C)} = \frac{0.3}{0.7} \approx 0.4286.$$

Posterior odds multiply by L:

$$\text{posterior odds} = \frac{P(V \mid r_1, r_2)}{P(C \mid r_1, r_2)} \approx 0.4286 \times 0.111 \approx 0.0476.$$

Hence

$$P(V \mid r_1, r_2) = \frac{0.0476}{1 + 0.0476} \approx 0.045.$$

So

$$P(V \mid r_1, r_2) \approx 0.045, \quad P(C \mid r_1, r_2) \approx 0.955.$$

For (b), r_3 given the regime is independent of r_1, r_2, with

$$\mathrm{Var}(r_3 \mid C) = 1, \quad \mathrm{Var}(r_3 \mid V) = 9,$$

and both conditional means are zero. The law of total variance gives

$$\mathrm{Var}(r_3 \mid r_1, r_2) = E[\mathrm{Var}(r_3 \mid \text{regime}) \mid r_1, r_2] + \mathrm{Var}(E[r_3 \mid \text{regime}] \mid r_1, r_2).$$

The second term is zero because $E[r_3 \mid C] = E[r_3 \mid V] = 0$. Thus

$$\mathrm{Var}(r_3 \mid r_1, r_2) = P(C \mid r_1, r_2) \cdot 1 + P(V \mid r_1, r_2) \cdot 9$$

$$\approx 0.955 \cdot 1 + 0.045 \cdot 9 \approx 0.955 + 0.405 \approx 1.36.$$

So the predictive variance is about 1.36.

For (c), if r_1 were huge in absolute value, say $r_1 = 0.08$, that observation is far more likely under the high-variance regime V than under C. Its likelihood ratio would be much larger than 1, so $P(V \mid r_1)$ would jump up significantly. Now consider a subsequent very small r_2, say -0.002. Such a tiny move is relatively more probable under the low-variance regime C than under V, so the likelihood ratio for day 2 alone would be less than 1 and would push the posterior back toward C.

The key point is that $P(V \mid r_1, r_2)$ is built up multiplicatively from the day-by-day likelihood ratios. The first extreme move increases the odds of V, but the second calm move partially undoes that by providing evidence for C. This is more subtle than a slogan like "large moves imply a volatile regime" because the posterior depends on the entire

84

sequence, not just some aggregate measure of volatility. Each new data point re-weights the regime probabilities through its own likelihood contribution.

Common Mistake: A frequent error is to look only at the magnitude of returns and think in terms of a single "overall volatility" estimate, ignoring the explicit regime model. Candidates often forget to compute the full joint likelihood under each regime and to use Bayes' rule with the correct prior odds. Another common slip in (b) is to take a simple weighted average of standard deviations instead of variances, or to forget that the mean is zero so the between-regime variance term vanishes. In (c), many people incorrectly assume that once an extreme r_1 occurs, the regime is essentially locked into V, missing the fact that subsequent observations still meaningfully update the posterior.

5.1.4: Question 5.4

Question: You are evaluating a new high-frequency signal that is either truly profitable (state A) or not (state N). Prior: $P(A) = 0.1$.

Each day you run a **binary** profitability test on the signal, which outputs either "pass" (P) or "fail" (F). The test is noisy but stable over time: - If A is true: $P(P \mid A) = 0.7$, $P(F \mid A) = 0.3$. - If N is true: $P(P \mid N) = 0.2$, $P(F \mid N) = 0.8$.

Assume the true state (A or N) is fixed over time and, conditional on the state, daily test outcomes are independent.

You observe 5 consecutive test outcomes: P, F, P, P, F.

(a) Compute the posterior probability that the signal is truly profitable, P(A | P, F, P, P, F).

(b) Suppose instead you only knew the **total count** of passes over 5 days was 3 (but not the exact sequence). Would the posterior probability P(A | 3 passes out of 5) be different from the answer in (a)? Explain why or why not.

(c) Conceptually, if you extended this to many days T and observed k passes, give the form of the likelihood ratio (up to a constant) in favor of A vs N, and explain how the law of large numbers shapes your posterior as T grows.

Answer: For (a), the likelihoods are $P(\text{seq} \mid A) = 0.7^3 0.3^2$, $P(\text{seq} \mid N) = 0.2^3 0.8^2$. The likelihood ratio is $L = \frac{0.7^3 0.3^2}{0.2^3 0.8^2} \approx 6.03$. Prior odds are $0.1/0.9 = 1/9$. Posterior odds are $(1/9) \cdot 6.03 \approx 0.669$, so $P(A \mid \text{data}) = \frac{0.669}{1+0.669} \approx 0.40$.

For (b), order does not matter because of independence and identical daily probabilities; only the counts $k = 3, T = 5$ matter. Thus $P(A \mid 3 \text{ passes})$ is the same as in (a).

For (c), with T days and k passes, $L_T(k) = \frac{0.7^k 0.3^{T-k}}{0.2^k 0.8^{T-k}} = (0.7/0.2)^k (0.3/0.8)^{T-k}$. By the law of large numbers, $k/T \to 0.7$ if A is true and $k/T \to 0.2$ if N is true, so $\log L_T$ grows linearly with T with positive drift under the true state, driving the posterior to 1 for the true state and 0 for the false one.

5.1.5: Question 5.5

Question: You are assessing whether a stock is currently overvalued (state O) or fairly valued (state F). Prior: $P(O) = 0.4$, $P(F) = 0.6$. Two conditionally independent teams give binary reports (V^+/V^-, M^+/M^-) with given accuracies. You observe V^+ and M^-.

- (a) Compute $P(O \mid V^+, M^-)$.
- (b) Change only the momentum behavior under F so that $P(M^+ \mid F) = 0.55$, $P(M^- \mid F) = 0.45$; recompute $P(O \mid V^+, M^-)$.
- (c) Intuitively compare the two posteriors and explain why degrading specificity under F raises $P(O \mid V^+, M^-)$.

Intuition: We are combining a prior belief about overvaluation with two noisy signals. Each signal's value comes from how differently it behaves under O versus F. Once we change the momentum team so they shout "negative" too often in fairly valued states, seeing "not negative" (M^-) actually becomes rarer under F and therefore relatively more supportive of O. So the same observed pair V^+, M^- will push us more toward O in the biased model.

Solution: With conditional independence,

$$P(O \mid V^+, M^-) = \frac{P(V^+, M^- \mid O)P(O)}{P(V^+, M^- \mid O)P(O) + P(V^+, M^- \mid F)P(F)}.$$

First model. Under O:

$$P(V^+, M^- \mid O) = P(V^+ \mid O)P(M^- \mid O) = 0.8 \cdot 0.4 = 0.32.$$

Under F:
$$P(V^+, M^- \mid F) = P(V^+ \mid F)P(M^- \mid F) = 0.3 \cdot 0.6 = 0.18.$$
Now,
$$\text{num} = 0.32 \cdot 0.4 = 0.128, \quad \text{den} = 0.128 + 0.18 \cdot 0.6$$
$$= 0.128 + 0.108 = 0.236,$$
so
$$P(O \mid V^+, M^-) = \frac{0.128}{0.236} \approx 0.542.$$

Biased momentum under F. Under O nothing changes, so joint likelihood is still 0.32. Under F we now have
$$P(M^- \mid F) = 1 - 0.55 = 0.45,$$
$$P(V^+, M^- \mid F) = 0.3 \cdot 0.45 = 0.135.$$
Thus
$$\text{num} = 0.32 \cdot 0.4 = 0.128, \quad \text{den} = 0.128 + 0.135 \cdot 0.6$$
$$= 0.128 + 0.081 = 0.209,$$
so
$$P(O \mid V^+, M^-) = \frac{0.128}{0.209} \approx 0.612.$$

Logic: Initially, M^- is more common under F than under O (0.6 vs 0.4), so it leans slightly toward F. After the bias, M^- becomes less common under F (0.45) while staying 0.4 under O. The likelihood ratio for M^- moves toward O:
$$\frac{P(M^- \mid O)}{P(M^- \mid F)} : \frac{0.4}{0.6} \approx 0.67 \quad \rightarrow \quad \frac{0.4}{0.45} \approx 0.89.$$
So M^- is now less of an argument for F, making the combined evidence V⁺, M⁻ more pro-O.

Common Mistake: People focus on the verbal label "not negative momentum" and assume it is always favorable to F. The correct approach is to look at how the probabilities change under each state. The information content comes from the relative likelihoods under O and F, not from the semantic meaning of "negative" versus "not negative."

5.1.6: Question 5.6

Question: You are modeling daily P&L of a high-frequency strategy. You have a long history and find: - Sample mean is close to 0. - Sample variance is stable over time. - However, the empirical kurtosis is around 10, far above 3.

A senior quant suggests using a normal distribution. You are not convinced.

(a) Give two distributions with same mean and variance but very different kurtosis and explain tail behavior.

(b) Explain why matching only mean and variance can be misleading, even with the CLT.

(c) Between Model A: Normal(0, σ^2) and Model B: symmetric Student-t with same variance, give one quantitative and one qualitative reason to prefer B for stress tests.

Answer:

(a) Let $X \sim N(0,1)$ (mean 0, variance 1, kurtosis 3). Define Y as a mixture: with prob 0.99, $Y \sim N(0, 1/0.99)$; with prob 0.01, $Y \sim N(0, 100/0.99)$. Then $E[Y] = 0$ and $\text{Var}(Y) = 1$, but kurtosis of Y is much larger than 3 because of the rare, very high-variance component. X has thin, exponentially decaying tails; Y produces extreme values far more often despite identical mean and variance.

(b) Risk is driven by tail losses, not typical fluctuations. A Gaussian calibrated only to variance will assign astronomically small probabilities to large moves. For $N(0,1)$, $P(|X| > 5) \approx 5.7 \times 10^{-7}$, whereas a heavy-tailed law with the same variance (like Y or a low-df t) can have $P(|X| > 5)$ orders of magnitude higher. CLT arguments concern sums under ideal conditions and justify the center of the distribution as horizons grow, not single-day extremes. Microstructure effects, volatility bursts, and dependence can all break the Gaussian approximation exactly where risk matters: large one-day drawdowns, margin calls, and liquidity crises.

(c) Quantitatively, choose a 5σ daily loss threshold. Under Model A, $X \sim N(0, \sigma^2)$, $P(X < -5\sigma) \approx 2.9 \times 10^{-7}$. Under Model B, say a standardized t_ν with $\nu = 5$ and variance matched to σ^2, $P(X < -5\sigma)$ is roughly 10^{-4}–10^{-3}, hundreds to thousands of times larger, even though both models share the same variance. For stress tests, underestimating this probability by such factors is unacceptable.

Qualitatively, high-frequency P&L is exposed to rare microstructure breakdowns, sudden liquidity gaps, exchange halts, and fat-finger events. These generate outliers far more frequently than a normal model allows. A symmetric Student-t keeps the central bulk similar to Gaussian but realistically inflates tail risk, making it more appropriate for capital, margin, and worst-case scenario analysis.

5.1.7: Question 5.7

Question: You model the **daily trade count** of a low-frequency discretionary strategy. Let N be the number of trades per day.

Historically, you estimate: - $E[N] \approx 4$ trades/day, - $Var(N) \approx 12$ trades^2/day^2.

  (a) Explain why a Poisson model for N is inconsistent with these empirical moments, and what *overdispersion* means in this context.

  (b) You consider a Negative Binomial model NB(r, p) for N, with mean $\mu = r(1-p)/p$ and variance $\mu + \mu^2/r$. Use the empirical mean and variance to solve for r (you can leave p implicit) and interpret what the estimated r tells you about the variability of daily trading intensity.

  (c) Give a plausible **financial interpretation** for why trade counts might be overdispersed relative to Poisson (i.e., why $Var(N) \gg E[N]$) in this setting, and why a mixture-of-Poissons story is natural here.

Answer: For Poisson with parameter λ, $E[N] = Var(N) = \lambda$. Empirically $E[N] \approx 4$ and $Var(N) \approx 12$, so variance is much larger than the mean, contradicting the Poisson property. This excess variance is called overdispersion: $Var(N) > E[N]$.

Using the Negative Binomial, set $\mu = 4$ and $12 = \mu + \mu^2 / r$. Then $12 = 4 + 16 / r$, so $8 = 16 / r$ and $r = 2$. A small r means strong extra variability and a heavy right tail; as $r \to \infty$, the model approaches Poisson.

Financially, daily trading intensity is not constant: some days (news, volatility, strong signals) have high latent intensity, others very low. If $N \mid \Lambda \sim$ Poisson(Λ) and Λ is random across days (e.g., Gamma), the unconditional N is Negative Binomial, naturally generating $Var(N) \gg E[N]$ via a mixture-of-Poissons mechanism.

5.1.8: Question 5.8

Question: You are combining two daily return streams X and Y from different strategies into a portfolio. Empirically, you estimate: $E[X] = E[Y] = 0$, $Var(X) = Var(Y) = 1$, $Corr(X, Y) \approx 0$. However, you also observe that large negative realizations tend to coincide: when $X < -3$, Y is often also very negative. Marginally, both X and Y look roughly symmetric and light-tailed; the issue is in the joint extremes.

(a) Explain how it is possible for $Corr(X, Y) \approx 0$ while large negative events tend to co-occur. What feature of the joint distribution is not captured by correlation here?

(b) Consider a portfolio return $R = X + Y$. Under a naive model where (X, Y) are independent $N(0,1)$, compute $Var(R)$ and $\mathbb{P}(R < -4)$.

(c) Now suppose that the marginals of X and Y are still $N(0,1)$, but the joint distribution has stronger lower-tail dependence than a bivariate normal with zero correlation. Without detailed copula math, argue qualitatively how $\mathbb{P}(R < -4)$ under this tail-dependent model compares to the naive Gaussian-independent model, even though $Var(R)$ is still 2 under both.

(d) From a risk-management perspective, explain why focusing only on covariance and variance when building portfolios of strategies can lead to dangerous underestimation of joint crash risk.

Intuition: Correlation averages co-movement over all days. Strong dependence that appears only in rare joint crashes can be "washed out" and still yield correlation near zero. The missing concept is tail dependence: how likely one leg is extreme given the other is extreme. This matters a lot for crash risk of $R = X + Y$ even when variances and covariances look benign.

Solution: For (a), correlation is

$$Corr(X,Y) = \frac{Cov(X,Y)}{\sqrt{Var(X)Var(Y)}} = \mathbb{E}[XY],$$

since $E[X] = E[Y] = 0$ and $Var(X) = Var(Y) = 1$. If mild positive and negative co-movements across most of the distribution cancel out, $\mathbb{E}[XY]$ can be close to zero. This does not rule out strong dependence restricted to a tiny region such as $\{X < -3, Y \ll 0\}$. The feature not captured is lower-tail dependence: $\mathbb{P}(Y$ very negative | X very negative).

For (b), under independent $N(0,1)$:

$$Var(R) = Var(X + Y) = Var(X) + Var(Y) + 2Cov(X,Y)$$
$$= 1 + 1 + 0 = 2.$$

Thus $R \sim N(0,2)$, so

$$\mathbb{P}(R < -4) = \mathbb{P}\left(Z < \frac{-4}{\sqrt{2}}\right) = \mathbb{P}(Z < -2\sqrt{2}),$$

with $Z \sim N(0,1)$. Numerically $-2\sqrt{2} \approx -2.828$, giving a probability around 0.0024 (about 0.24%).

For (c), the marginals remain $N(0,1)$, so $Var(X) = Var(Y) = 1$ and still

$$Var(R) = 1 + 1 + 2Cov(X,Y) = 2,$$

since correlation is still near zero. But stronger lower-tail dependence means that when X is very negative, Y is more likely to also be very negative than in the independent Gaussian case. That shifts probability mass into outcomes where R is very negative (e.g. $R < -4$), while compensating by reducing probability in moderate outcomes, so the overall variance stays 2. Therefore,

$$\mathbb{P}(R < -4)_{\text{tail-dependent}} > \mathbb{P}(R < -4)_{\text{indep. Gaussian}}.$$

For (d), if you only look at variance and covariance, you are effectively assuming something like a Gaussian or elliptical world where dependence is fully summarized by correlation. In reality, strategies can be weakly correlated on normal days but share hidden exposures that only show up in stress (liquidity squeezes, crowded trades, macro shocks). Mean-variance optimization will then label them as diversifying, overweight them, and dramatically underestimate the probability and size of joint crashes. Ignoring tail dependence and joint extreme scenarios leads to portfolios that look safe in covariance space but are fragile in crises.

Common Mistake: Many candidates implicitly assume that "low correlation" guarantees good diversification everywhere, including in extremes. They forget that variance is a second-moment summary and that correlation does not describe how dependence behaves in the tails, where risk management actually cares most.

5.1.9: Question 5.9

Question: You are fitting a distribution to **monthly equity index returns**. From a long historical sample, you estimate: - Mean ≈ 0.7% per month, - Standard deviation ≈ 4% per month, - Sample skewness ≈ −0.8 (moderately negative), - Sample kurtosis ≈ 5 (heavier tails than Gaussian).

(a) Explain qualitatively what the **negative skewness** and **excess kurtosis** imply about the shape of the return distribution relative to a normal distribution with the same mean and variance.

(b) Give one concrete risk metric (based on a tail probability or quantile) that will be **materially misestimated** by the normal model, and indicate in which direction (too high or too low) the normal model's estimate will be compared to reality.

(c) Suggest a more appropriate parametric family (or modeling approach) for these returns that can accommodate both skewness and heavy tails, and briefly justify why it is more suitable in this context.

Answer: (a) Negative skewness (−0.8) means the left tail is longer/fatter: large negative returns are more likely than equally large positive returns, relative to a symmetric normal. Kurtosis ≈ 5 (>3) means heavier tails and a sharper peak: more extreme outcomes in both tails and more mass near the mean, with less in the mid-range. Together, compared with N(0.7%, 4), there are more frequent and more severe crashes.

    (b) A 1% monthly left-tail Value-at-Risk. Under normality, $VaR_{1\%} \approx 0.7\% + 4\% \cdot \Phi^{-1}(0.01) \approx 0.7\% - 9.3\% \approx -8.6\%$. The true 1% quantile is more negative, so the normal model underestimates downside risk (VaR is too high / too optimistic).

    (c) A skewed Student-t distribution is more suitable: it adds a skew parameter to capture asymmetric left tail and a degrees-of-freedom parameter to generate heavy tails, matching both the negative skewness and excess kurtosis observed in equity returns.

5.1.10: Question 5.10

Question: You are comparing two candidate models for a daily return R of a crypto asset, both centered at zero for simplicity:

- Model G: $R \sim N(0, \sigma^2)$ (Gaussian).
- Model H: R has a symmetric heavy-tailed distribution with pdf proportional to $1 / (1 + r^2)^{\{\alpha/2\}}$ for some $\alpha > 2$ (a Student-t-type tail), scaled so that $Var(R) = \sigma^2$.

    (a) For Model G, write down the moment generating function (MGF) M_G(t) and its radius of convergence. Comment on what this implies about the existence of all moments.

    (b) For Model H, argue qualitatively why the MGF M_H(t) = E[e^{tR}] may not exist (i.e., be finite) for any t ≠ 0 when α is not too large, even though the variance is finite. What does this say about the growth of the tails relative to the exponential function?

(c) Explain why the **central limit theorem** can still apply to sums of i.i.d. returns under Model H (for suitable α), even if the MGF does not exist, and what conditions on α are relevant.

(d) From a modeling perspective, discuss one **practical implication** of using a model like H (with possibly non-existent MGF) for risk calculations that involve exponentials, such as pricing of lognormal-like payoffs or computing $E[e^{\lambda R}]$.

Answer: For Model G, the MGF is $M\_G(t) = E[e^{tR}] = \exp(\frac{1}{2}\sigma^2 t^2)$, finite for all real t, so the radius of convergence is infinite and all moments of every order exist via derivatives at $t = 0$.

For Model H, the pdf has tails like $c/|r|^{\alpha}$. Then in $M\_H(t) = \int e^{tr} f(r)dr$, the factor e^{tr} grows exponentially, while f(r) decays only polynomially. Exponential growth dominates polynomial decay, so for any $t \neq 0$ one tail makes the integral diverge, even though $E[R^2]$ is finite for α > 2.

The CLT only requires finite variance (and mild regularity), not an MGF. If α > 2 so Var(R) < ∞, normalized sums still converge in distribution to N(0,1).

Practically, with such heavy tails, expectations like $E[e^{\lambda R}]$ or prices of $e^{\lambda R}$-type payoffs may be infinite or extremely unstable, so lognormal-based pricing formulas or risk measures that rely on exponential moments can fail or severely misestimate risk.

Chapter 6: Statistical Estimation and Inference Intuition

In quantitative work, we are paid—not for having data—but for drawing believable conclusions from incomplete, noisy data. Statistical estimation and inference are the craft tools for doing exactly that: turning a messy, finite sample of returns into disciplined statements about the unknown "truth" that generated them. The core questions are surprisingly human: given what I've seen, what should I believe, how uncertain should I be, and what risks do I run if I'm wrong?

Imagine you are evaluating a new trading strategy. You observe twelve months of live returns and compute an average monthly return of 1.2%. It is tempting to declare victory and annualize this number. But that average is a point estimate: a single guess for an unknown quantity, the true expected return. If you restarted the world 1,000 times, re-ran the same strategy for twelve months in each universe, and recomputed the sample average each time, you would not get the same answer. Some universes would make you look like a genius; others might make you look reckless. The pattern formed by those hypothetical averages is where bias and variance live: do your estimates tend, on average, to be too high or too low, and how wildly do they fluctuate from sample to sample?

Much of statistical practice can be viewed as navigating this bias–variance trade-off. A very flexible estimator can contort itself to fit the data you happened to see—perfectly matching the past at the cost of being fragile in the future. A more rigid estimator might be "wrong" in some systematic way, but change less across samples. Shrinkage techniques, Bayesian priors, and even simple rules like using longer lookback windows for volatility are all ways of quietly trading off variance for bias. One curious fact in finance is that the seemingly innocent sample Sharpe ratio you compute for a strategy is not just noisy—it is typically upward biased, especially when the sample is short. The very strategies that look most appealing in backtests often owe part of their charm to estimation error.

Because a single point estimate hides this uncertainty, we often wrap it in a confidence interval, a range of plausible values for the unknown quantity. When you say, "I estimate my strategy's annualized volatility at 15%, plus or minus 3%," you are implicitly acknowledging that the same strategy, in a parallel world, might have produced data that led you to 13% or 17% instead. A deeper, and at first slightly paradoxical, insight is that the interval is not random after you've computed it—the data have already spoken. What is random is the process that generated both the data and the interval. Over many hypothetical repetitions, intervals constructed this way would capture the true volatility a pre-specified fraction of the time. This long-run frequency interpretation underpins much of classical inference in practice, even when practitioners talk as if they had a probability distribution over "the true Sharpe ratio."

The bridge between the data and these inferential statements is often built from likelihood. Likelihood is a way of asking, "If the true mean return were 0% vs. 5%, how consistent are these observed returns with each possibility?" You can think of it as a scoring rule for different candidate worlds: the world in which your parameters are closest to the truth makes the observed data look relatively unsurprising. Maximizing the likelihood—choosing the parameters that make what you saw least surprising—is a remarkably general principle. It sits quietly beneath ubiquitous tools in quant finance, from fitting GARCH models for volatility to calibrating factor models and estimating risk premia.

Once you can compare how plausible different parameter values are, it is natural to extend this reasoning to hypotheses about models themselves. Does this new factor truly add explanatory power for returns, or is it just an illusion born of noisy data and extensive searching? Hypothesis testing gives you a structured way to ask, "How extreme are these results, relative to what I'd typically see if there were actually no effect?" In the context of Sharpe ratios, this might mean asking whether a backtested Sharpe of 1.0 is meaningfully different from zero after accounting for sample length and volatility clustering. In volatility estimation, it might mean checking whether an apparent drop in risk after a regime change is large enough to be statistically credible, or merely a calm-looking patch within a fundamentally unchanged storm.

An intriguing and often underappreciated aspect of inference in quantitative finance is how inherently conditional it is. We estimate expected returns and volatilities not in a vacuum, but conditional on models that are at best approximations: normality assumptions, independence across time, or linear factor structures. It is entirely possible for an estimation procedure to be mathematically impeccable and practically misleading if the underlying model is badly misspecified. This is one reason experienced quants are wary of taking p-values or confidence intervals at face value; they read them as signals that live within a broader, model-uncertain reality.

In this chapter, we will unpack these ideas not as abstract statistics, but through the lens of estimating returns, volatility, and Sharpe ratios—the everyday bread and butter of a working quant. Along the way you will see why the "obvious" estimators you learned early on are sometimes fragile, how thoughtfully adding a bit of bias can reduce risk, and how to interpret those ubiquitous intervals and test statistics in a way that aligns with real-world decision making. The destination is intuition: to look at a noisy performance track record and develop a disciplined sense of what it truly supports, what it only suggests, and what it absolutely does not justify believing.

6.1: Interview Questions

6.1.1: Question 6.1

Question: You are evaluating a new intraday trading signal. Historically, across thousands of backtests at your firm, only 5% of proposed signals are genuinely profitable out-of-sample; the other 95% are effectively noise.

For any genuinely profitable signal, your internal backtest framework flags it as "promising" 90% of the time (10% false negatives). For a noise signal, the system still flags it as "promising" 20% of the time due to overfitting and multiple-testing effects (20% false positives).

You run the new signal through the framework and it is flagged as "promising".

(a) Compute the posterior probability that the signal is genuinely profitable.

(b) Now suppose you add a *second*, independent validation test with the same operating characteristics (90% true positive, 20% false positive) and the signal passes *both* tests. Compute the updated posterior probability.

(c) Explain, in words, why the base rate of 5% matters much more than the seemingly high 90% test accuracy when interpreting a single promising result.

Answer:

Let G = "genuinely profitable", P = "flagged promising".

(a) Prior: $P(G) = 0.05$, $P(G^c) = 0.95$. $P(P \mid G) = 0.9$, $P(P \mid G^c) = 0.2$.

$$P(G \mid P) = \frac{0.9 \cdot 0.05}{0.9 \cdot 0.05 + 0.2 \cdot 0.95} = \frac{0.045}{0.235} \approx 0.191$$

So about 19.1%.

(b) Two independent passes P_1, P_2:

$P(P_1, P_2 \mid G) = 0.9^2 = 0.81$, $P(P_1, P_2 \mid G^c) = 0.2^2 = 0.04$.

$$P(G \mid P_1, P_2) = \frac{0.81 \cdot 0.05}{0.81 \cdot 0.05 + 0.04 \cdot 0.95} = \frac{0.0405}{0.0785} \approx 0.516$$

So about 51.6%.

    (c) Because only 5% of signals are truly good, the pool is dominated by noise. With a 20% false positive rate applied to 95% noise, you get many more noisy signals labeled "promising" than truly good ones. Thus, after one "promising" result, the posterior is still low (~19%) despite the 90% sensitivity. The low base rate (prior) strongly pulls the posterior down; multiple independent confirmations are needed to overcome it.

6.1.2: Question 6.2

Question: You are modeling whether a stock is currently *undervalued* (U) or *fairly/over-valued* ($\neg U$). Prior: $P(U) = 0.3$. Signals A (cheap) and B (weak momentum) are conditionally independent given U or $\neg U$. Given: - $P(A = 1 \mid U) = 0.8$, $P(A = 1 \mid \neg U) = 0.3$ - $P(B = 1 \mid U) = 0.7$, $P(B = 1 \mid \neg U) = 0.4$

    (a) Compute $P(U \mid A = 1)$.

    (b) Then observe $B = 0$; compute $P(U \mid A = 1, B = 0)$.

    (c) Explain why updating with $(A = 1, B = 0)$ in one step gives the same posterior, and interpret the direction of the change from (a) to (b).

Intuition: You start with a 30% belief the stock is undervalued. Seeing it looks cheap ($A = 1$) should increase that belief. Then learning that momentum is not weak ($B = 0$) is mildly contrary to undervaluation, so it should pull the probability back down, but not all the way to the original prior. Because the signals are conditionally independent, it does not matter whether you update them sequentially or jointly; you end up with the same posterior.

Solution:

(a) Use Bayes' rule with $A = 1$:

$$P(U \mid A = 1) = \frac{P(A = 1 \mid U)P(U)}{P(A = 1 \mid U)P(U) + P(A = 1 \mid \neg U)P(\neg U)}.$$

Plugging in:

$$P(U \mid A = 1) = \frac{0.8 \cdot 0.3}{0.8 \cdot 0.3 + 0.3 \cdot 0.7} = \frac{0.24}{0.24 + 0.21} = \frac{0.24}{0.45}$$

$$\approx 0.533.$$

(b) First compute $P(B = 0 \mid U) = 1 - 0.7 = 0.3$ and $P(B = 0 \mid \neg U) = 1 - 0.4 = 0.6$. Treat $P(U \mid A = 1)$ as the new prior and update on $B = 0$:

$$P(U \mid A = 1, B = 0)$$

$$= \frac{P(B = 0 \mid U)P(U \mid A = 1)}{P(B = 0 \mid U)P(U \mid A = 1) + P(B = 0 \mid \neg U)P(\neg U \mid A = 1)}.$$

With $P(U \mid A = 1) \approx 0.533$, $P(\neg U \mid A = 1) \approx 0.467$:

$$P(U \mid A = 1, B = 0) \approx \frac{0.3 \cdot 0.533}{0.3 \cdot 0.533 + 0.6 \cdot 0.467}$$

$$= \frac{0.1599}{0.1599 + 0.2802} \approx \frac{0.1599}{0.4401} \approx 0.363.$$

(c) Joint updating uses:

$$P(U \mid A = 1, B = 0) \propto P(A = 1, B = 0 \mid U)P(U).$$

Conditional independence gives

$$P(A = 1, B = 0 \mid U) = P(A = 1 \mid U)P(B = 0 \mid U),$$

and similarly under $\neg U$. This factorization is exactly what sequential Bayes does: first multiply by $P(A = 1 \mid \cdot)$, then by $P(B = 0 \mid \cdot)$. Multiplication is commutative, so order does not matter, and the posterior must match the answer in (b).

From (a) to (b), your belief rises from 0.3 to about 0.533 after seeing "cheap," then falls to about 0.363 after seeing "not weak momentum," which is modestly against undervaluation. Each signal nudges probability in its own direction; the final 0.363 reflects both pieces of evidence.

Common Mistake: A frequent error is to ignore conditional independence and incorrectly add or average likelihoods instead of multiplying them, or to think that sequential and joint updating give different answers. Another subtle mistake is forgetting to update the complementary probability $P(\neg U \mid A = 1)$ before the second Bayes step, which leads to incorrect normalization.

6.1.3: Question 6.3

Question: You are evaluating whether a daily trading signal S has *positive* true alpha (H1) or *zero* alpha (H0). Your prior odds are $P(H1) : P(H0) = 1 : 9$ (i.e., prior probability of positive alpha is 10%).

You run a backtest and obtain a t-statistic T = 2.0 for the signal's mean return. Assume: - Under H0 (zero alpha), T $\sim N(0, 1)$. - Under H1 (positive alpha of the magnitude you care about), T $\sim N(\mu, 1)$ with $\mu = 2$.

   (a) Compute the likelihood ratio $\Lambda = f_1(T{=}2) / f_0(T{=}2)$, where f_1 and f_0 are the $N(2,1)$ and $N(0,1)$ densities respectively.

   (b) Use posterior odds = prior odds × likelihood ratio to compute the posterior probability $P(H_1 \mid T{=}2)$.

   (c) Explain the key intuitive reason why a t-stat of 2, often treated as "statistically significant" in classical testing, does *not* imply a very high posterior probability that the signal truly has positive alpha in this setup.

Answer: For a normal $N(m,1)$, $f(x) = \frac{1}{\sqrt{2\pi}} \exp\left(-\frac{(x-m)^2}{2}\right)$. At $T = 2$ under H_0: $f_0(2) \propto \exp(-4/2) = e^{-2}$. Under H_1: $f_1(2) \propto \exp(0) = 1$. Thus $\Lambda = f_1(2)/f_0(2) = e^2 \approx 7.39$. Prior odds for H_1 are $1{:}9$, so posterior odds are $(1/9) \cdot 7.39 \approx 0.821$. Hence $P(H_1 \mid T = 2) = 0.821/(1 + 0.821) \approx 0.45$. Intuitively, $T = 2$ is only moderately more likely under H_1 than H_0, while the prior strongly favors H_0. Classical "significance" ignores this low prior; Bayesian updating shows that with many weak signals and few real ones, $T = 2$ still leaves less than 50% belief in true positive alpha.

6.1.4: Question 6.4

Question: Your firm runs a daily risk-monitoring system on 1,000 trading books. For each book, the system classifies the day as either "stress" (S) or "normal" (N) based on intraday P&L patterns.

Historically, *true* stress days (large risk events) occur on only 2% of book-days. On a true stress day, the system correctly flags stress with probability 0.9. On a non-stress day, it falsely flags stress with probability 0.05.

(a) For a randomly chosen book on a randomly chosen day, the system flags "stress". Compute the posterior probability that this is actually a true stress day.

(b) Explain why, even though the system is quite accurate in terms of true positive and false positive rates, the majority of stress alerts may still be false alarms. Relate your explanation to how a risk manager should interpret an individual alert.

(c) Suppose a risk manager informally claims: "If the system says stress, I'm 90% sure it's really stress". Which specific probabilistic quantity are they confusing with the posterior probability you computed in (a)?

Answer:

(a) Let E = true stress day, A = system flags stress. $P(E) = 0.02$, $P(E^c) = 0.98$, $P(A \mid E) = 0.9$, $P(A \mid E^c) = 0.05$.

$$P(E \mid A) = \frac{P(A \mid E)P(E)}{P(A \mid E)P(E) + P(A \mid E^c)P(E^c)}$$

$$= \frac{0.9 \cdot 0.02}{0.9 \cdot 0.02 + 0.05 \cdot 0.98} = \frac{0.018}{0.067} \approx 0.269.$$

So about 27%.

Intuition: Because true stress days are very rare, even a small false-positive rate on the many non-stress days creates many false alerts. The system greatly increases the probability from 2% to about 27%, but a single alert is far from conclusive; it signals "elevated risk," not "near certainty." A risk manager should treat an alert as a strong warning that needs further investigation, not as a 90% confirmation.

Misinterpretation in (c): The manager is confusing the sensitivity $P(A \mid E) = 0.9$ (probability the system flags stress given true stress) with the posterior $P(E \mid A)$ (probability of true stress given a stress flag).

6.1.5: Question 6.5

Question: A PM runs a relatively low-turnover equity strategy. Each month you classify the realized performance as either "outperformed benchmark" (+) or "underperformed" (−), after adjusting for risk and noise. You are trying to infer whether the PM has genuine skill (S) or is unskilled (U).

Your prior belief is $P(S) = 0.2$, $P(U) = 0.8$.

Conditional on S or U, the monthly outcomes are independent with: If S (skilled): $P(+) = 0.6$, $P(-) = 0.4$. If U (unskilled): $P(+) = 0.5$, $P(-) = 0.5$.

You observe a run of 4 months: +, +, −, +.

  (a) Compute the posterior probability $P(S \mid \text{data})$ after observing these 4 months.

  (b) Without redoing the full calculation, explain how the posterior would change qualitatively if the sequence had been +, +, +, + instead. Focus your reasoning on likelihood ratios or Bayes factors.

  (c) Interpret your result from (a) in terms of whether you would be comfortable substantially increasing the PM's capital allocation purely based on this 4-

month track record. Emphasize the role of prior belief and the modest difference between skilled and unskilled outcome probabilities.

Intuition:

We are updating a prior belief about "skilled vs unskilled" using Bayes' rule. The evidence is the pattern of monthly pluses and minuses. Skill slightly tilts the win probability from 0.5 to 0.6, so over only four months the patterns you see are not that different under S versus U. The posterior will move, but not dramatically, because both the prior is skeptical and the likelihoods are fairly close.

Solution:

Let D be the observed sequence $+, +, -, +$.

Under S, wins have probability 0.6 and losses 0.4, independent month to month. The likelihood is

$$P(D \mid S) = 0.6^3 \cdot 0.4^1 = 0.216 \cdot 0.4 = 0.0864.$$

Under U, each month is 0.5 for $+$ or $-$, so

$$P(D \mid U) = 0.5^4 = 0.0625.$$

Using Bayes' rule with priors $P(S) = 0.2$, $P(U) = 0.8$,

$$P(S \mid D) = \frac{P(D \mid S)P(S)}{P(D \mid S)P(S) + P(D \mid U)P(U)}.$$

Compute the numerator and denominator:

$$P(D, S) = 0.0864 \cdot 0.2 = 0.01728,$$

$$P(D, U) = 0.0625 \cdot 0.8 = 0.05,$$

$$P(S \mid D) = \frac{0.01728}{0.01728 + 0.05} = \frac{0.01728}{0.06728} \approx 0.257.$$

So the posterior probability of skill after observing $+, +, -, +$ is about 25.7%.

For part (b), consider $D' = +, +, +, +$. Then

$$P(D' \mid S) = 0.6^4 = 0.1296, \quad P(D' \mid U) = 0.5^4 = 0.0625.$$

The Bayes factor is the likelihood ratio. For D,

$$BF_D = \frac{P(D \mid S)}{P(D \mid U)} = \frac{0.0864}{0.0625} \approx 1.382.$$

For D',

$$BF_{D'} = \frac{P(D' \mid S)}{P(D' \mid U)} = \frac{0.1296}{0.0625} \approx 2.074.$$

Because $BF_{D'} > BF_D$, the all-+ sequence provides stronger evidence in favor of S than $+, +, -, +$ does. Starting from the same prior $P(S) = 0.2$, multiplying the prior odds by $BF_{D'}$ instead of BF_D would give a higher posterior for S. Qualitatively, the posterior for S would be meaningfully above 25.7%, but still far from near-certain, because the skill edge is modest and the sample is very short.

Logic:

The algorithmic logic is: first compute, under each hypothesis S and U, how likely the observed sequence is by multiplying the appropriate monthly probabilities. Then weight those likelihoods by the prior probabilities of S and U. Finally normalize to get posterior probabilities that sum to 1. For comparing different sequences, you do not need to redo all arithmetic; you just compare likelihood ratios $P(\text{data} \mid S)/P(\text{data} \mid U)$, because the prior stays the same and the posterior odds equal prior odds times this ratio.

Common Mistake:

A frequent mistake is to overreact to "three wins out of four" and ignore the prior and the modest skill edge. Many candidates intuitively jump to "this looks pretty skilled" without quantifying how similar the pattern is under an unskilled 0.5 process. Another error is to look only at $P(D \mid S)$ and forget that Bayes' rule compares it to $P(D \mid U)$; a high $P(D \mid S)$ alone does not mean much if $P(D \mid U)$ is also high. Here, even after four mostly positive months, the posterior still says "more likely unskilled," so a large capital increase based purely on this short run would not be justified.

6.1.6: Question 6.6

Question: You are modeling daily P&L of a trading strategy as a mixture of two regimes: - Normal regime (N): returns are $N(0, 1^2)$ with probability 0.9. - Stress regime (S): returns are $N(0, 5^2)$ with probability 0.1.

Assume which regime occurs each day is independent across days.

(a) Compute the mean and variance of the *unconditional* daily return distribution.

(b) Without computing any integrals, argue whether the unconditional distribution has heavier or lighter tails than a single normal distribution with the same variance you found in (a).

(c) Suppose a colleague insists on fitting a single normal $N(0, \hat{\sigma}^2)$ to the data using sample variance. Explain qualitatively how this misspecification will affect 1-day 99% VaR estimates compared to the true mixture model.

Answer:

(a) Let R be return. $E[R] = 0.9 \cdot 0 + 0.1 \cdot 0 = 0$.
$\text{Var}(R) = E[\text{Var}(R \mid \text{regime})] + \text{Var}(E[R \mid \text{regime}]) = 0.9 \cdot 1^2 + 0.1 \cdot 5^2 + 0 = 0.9 + 2.5 = 3.4$.

(b) The mixture is $0.9\,N(0,1) + 0.1\,N(0,25)$. Around zero, the low-variance $N(0,1)$ dominates, so it is more peaked than $N(0,3.4)$. In the tails, the $N(0,25)$ component dominates, giving larger tail probabilities. Hence the mixture has heavier tails than $N(0,3.4)$.

(c) Fitting $N(0,\hat{\sigma}^2)$ with $\hat{\sigma}^2 \approx 3.4$ matches variance but not tail heaviness. A single normal with variance 3.4 decays too fast in the tails, so the 1% lower quantile (99% VaR) is not negative enough. The normal fit will underestimate true 1-day 99% VaR, thus understating tail risk from stress days.

6.1.7: Question 6.7

Question: You are evaluating two trading strategies A and B with *zero* expected daily return but different payoff shapes.

- Strategy A: Each day, with probability 0.99 you earn +1, and with probability 0.01 you lose −99.
- Strategy B: Each day, with probability 0.5 you earn +5, and with probability 0.5 you lose −5.

Assume independent daily outcomes.

(a) Verify that both strategies have zero expected daily return and compute their daily variances.

(b) A risk-averse PM prefers B over A even though the means and (surprisingly) the variances turn out to be equal. Explain what feature of the distributions makes A intuitively much more dangerous in a risk management context.

(c) Suppose you are forced to summarize each strategy by *one* scalar risk metric to feed into an optimization. Suggest a metric (other than variance) that would distinguish A from B in the desired direction and justify your choice in terms of tail behavior or higher moments.

Answer: (a) For A, let daily P&L be X_A. $E[X_A] = 0.99 \cdot 1 + 0.01 \cdot (-99) = 0.99 - 0.99 = 0$. $E[X_A^2] = 0.99 \cdot 1^2 + 0.01 \cdot (-99)^2 = 0.99 + 0.01 \cdot 9801 = 99$. $\mathrm{Var}(X_A) = 99 - 0^2 = 99$.

For B, X_B: $E[X_B] = 0.5 \cdot 5 + 0.5 \cdot (-5) = 0$. $E[X_B^2] = 0.5 \cdot 5^2 + 0.5 \cdot (-5)^2 = 25$. $\mathrm{Var}(X_B) = 25$.

(b) Strategy A has extreme negative skewness: many small gains but rare, huge crashes (heavy left tail). This "lottery-like" crash risk is far more dangerous for drawdowns and solvency than B's symmetric, moderate fluctuations, even if variance were matched.

(c) A good scalar metric is a tail-risk measure such as high-quantile Expected Shortfall (e.g., 99% ES). For A, ES heavily reflects the −99 crash; for B, tail losses are only −5. ES explicitly focuses on downside tail behavior and will rank A as much riskier than B despite equal mean or even equal variance.

6.1.8: Question 6.8

Question: You are modeling the 1-month *price* of a stock, $S(1)$, given today's price $S(0) = 100$. A junior analyst proposes to model $S(1)$ as Normal(μ, σ^2) directly. You instead propose to model the *log-return* $R = \ln(S(1)/S(0))$ as Normal(m, v), so that $S(1)$ is lognormal.

(a) Give two concrete reasons, based on properties of the distributions, why modeling log-returns as normal is usually more sensible than modeling prices as normal.

(b) Under the lognormal model, express $E[S(1)]$ and $\text{Var}(S(1)]$ in terms of $S(0)$, m, and v.

(c) In practice, daily log-returns are not exactly normal. Name one stylized empirical feature of returns that contradicts the simple lognormal model, and explain briefly what kind of distributional modification could capture it.

Answer: Modeling prices as normal allows $S(1) < 0$ with positive probability, which is impossible, while a lognormal $S(1)$ is strictly positive. Also, returns compound multiplicatively; log-returns add over time, so normal log-returns give time-consistent aggregation of returns, unlike normal prices.

With $R \sim N(m, v)$ and $S(1) = S(0)e^R$, $E[S(1)] = S(0) e^{m+v/2}$ and $\text{Var}(S(1)) = S(0)^2 e^{2m+v} (e^v - 1)$.

Empirically, returns show heavy tails (excess kurtosis), with more extreme moves than normality implies. This can be captured by using, for example, a Student-t distribution or a normal mixture / stochastic volatility model for returns.

6.1.9: Question 6.9

Question: You are comparing two daily trading strategies C and D with the same true mean μ and variance σ^2 of daily returns, but different higher moments. C is approximately normal; D is symmetric, heavy-tailed (large $E[R^4]$). You estimate the Sharpe

$$\hat{S} = \frac{\bar{R}}{\hat{\sigma}}$$

from T i.i.d. daily returns.

(a) Which strategy has a more variable $\hat{S}$ across samples, and why?

(b) Why are heavy-tailed strategies more likely to appear at the top of a Sharpe ranking over many strategies, even if all have the same true Sharpe?

(c) Suggest a practical adjustment to reduce this bias without fully modeling each return distribution.

Intuition: Heavy tails mean occasional huge returns in magnitude. Those rare events make both the sample mean and sample volatility jump around much more between samples. Because $\hat{S}$ is a ratio of these two noisy quantities, its sampling distribution becomes much fatter for heavy-tailed strategies. When you then take the maximum across many strategies, the ones with fatter sampling tails are disproportionately likely to win by luck.

Solution: The variability of $\hat{S}$ depends on the joint sampling behavior of $\bar{R}$ and $\hat{\sigma}$. Asymptotically,

$$\sqrt{T}(\bar{R} - \mu) \xrightarrow{d} N(0, \sigma^2),$$

but the variance of $\hat{\sigma}^2$ and the covariance structure depend on the fourth central moment $E[(R - \mu)^4]$. For normal returns, $E[(R - \mu)^4] = 3\sigma^4$. For heavy-tailed D, $E[(R - \mu)^4] \gg 3\sigma^4$. This inflates

$$\text{Var}(\hat{\sigma}^2), \quad \text{Var}(\bar{R}), \quad \text{and hence } \text{Var}(\hat{S}).$$

Thus (a) strategy D has a more variable $\hat{S}$.

For (b), consider many strategies $\{i\}$ with identical true Sharpe S^*. Each has an estimate $\hat{S}_i$ with some sampling distribution. For heavy-tailed strategies, the distribution of $\hat{S}_i$ has fatter tails, so

$$P(\hat{S}_i > x) \quad \text{is larger for heavy-tailed i when x is large.}$$

When you take the maximum $\max_i \hat{S}_i$, you are selecting an extreme order statistic. The probability that this extreme comes from a distribution with fatter tails is higher. Therefore, the top-ranked strategy is more likely to be heavy-tailed and its Sharpe more likely to be an overestimate of S^*.

For (c), a practical adjustment is to use a robust Sharpe estimator that down-weights extremes, for example computing $\hat{S}$ on winsorized or trimmed returns: cap or cut the largest and smallest returns, then compute mean and standard deviation. This reduces the influence of rare huge moves, narrows the sampling distribution of $\hat{S}$ for heavy-tailed strategies, and thereby weakens the selection bias toward them.

Common Mistake: Many candidates focus only on mean and variance, assuming CLT makes everything "normal enough." They ignore the role of $E[R^4]$ in driving the sampling variability of $\hat{S}$ and miss that selection across many strategies amplifies these higher-moment effects.

6.1.10: Question 6.10

Question: A colleague proposes to model daily log-returns X of a crypto asset with a symmetric distribution that has power-law tails: for large x,

$$\mathbb{P}(|X| > x) \approx Cx^{-\alpha}$$

for some constants $C > 0$ and tail index $\alpha \in (1,3)$. You recall that for such distributions, higher moments may not exist.

   (a) For which values of α do the mean $\mathbb{E}[X]$ and variance $\text{Var}(X)$ exist? Express your answer as conditions on α.

   (b) Briefly explain why the moment generating function (mgf) $M_X(t) = \mathbb{E}[e^{tX}]$ typically does not exist (is infinite) for any nonzero t when X has such power-law tails, even if the mean and variance are finite.

   (c) Your risk system currently assumes returns are normal and uses the mgf to compute closed-form expressions for some risk metrics. You cannot easily rewrite the system. Suggest a sensible approximate modeling approach that preserves the heavy-tail behavior of X for risk purposes while still allowing you to use mgf-based formulas internally.

Intuition: Power-law tails decay too slowly for high moments. If $\mathbb{P}(|X| > x)$ behaves like $x^{-\alpha}$, then roughly the k-th moment exists only if $\alpha > k$. Exponential weighting in the mgf, via e^{tX}, grows much faster than any power, so polynomial tail decay cannot compensate and the mgf usually blows up.

Solution: For large x, use the tail-moment relation

$$\mathbb{E}[|X|^k] < \infty \quad \Leftrightarrow \quad \int_1^\infty x^k \, d\mathbb{P}(|X| \le x) < \infty.$$

With $\mathbb{P}(|X| > x) \approx Cx^{-\alpha}$, integration by parts or standard tail results give

$$\mathbb{E}[|X|^k] < \infty \quad \text{iff} \quad \alpha > k.$$

For the mean, $k = 1$. Symmetry gives $\mathbb{E}[X] = 0$ whenever $\mathbb{E}[|X|] < \infty$. Thus

$$\mathbb{E}[X] \text{ exists} \quad \Leftrightarrow \quad \alpha > 1.$$

For the variance, need $\mathbb{E}[X^2] < \infty$, so $k = 2$:

$$\text{Var}(X) \text{ exists} \quad \Leftrightarrow \quad \alpha > 2.$$

Given $\alpha \in (1,3)$, this yields: if $1 < \alpha \le 2$, the mean exists but the variance is infinite; if $2 < \alpha < 3$, both mean and variance exist, but higher moments (e.g. $k \ge 3$) may fail. For the mgf, consider $t > 0$. On the right tail,

$$\mathbb{E}[e^{tX}] \supset \int_K^\infty e^{tx} f(x) \, dx.$$

With a power-law tail, $f(x)$ decays like $x^{-(\alpha+1)}$ or similar. As $x \to \infty$, the integrand behaves like $e^{tx}x^{-(\alpha+1)}$, and e^{tx} dominates any polynomial decay. Hence

$$\int_K^\infty e^{tx} f(x)\, dx = \infty,$$

so $M_X(t) = \infty$ for all $t > 0$. By symmetry and the left tail, $M_X(t) = \infty$ also for all $t < 0$. This divergence occurs even if $\mathbb{E}[X]$ and $\mathbb{E}[X^2]$ are finite, because the mgf demands integrability under exponentially increasing weights, which is much stricter than finite low-order moments.

For risk-system compatibility, one sensible approximation is to replace X by a distribution with a finite mgf that still mimics heavy tails in relevant quantiles. A practical choice is a finite mixture of normals: let

$$X_{\text{approx}} \sim \sum_j p_j\, \mathcal{N}(\mu_j, \sigma_j^2),$$

with weights, means, and variances calibrated so that X_{approx} matches the empirical mean, variance, and key tail quantiles (for example 95% and 99% VaR) of the power-law data. Each normal component has mgf

$$M_j(t) = \exp\left(\mu_j t + 1/2\, \sigma_j^2 t^2\right),$$

and the mixture mgf is the finite sum $M_{X_{\text{approx}}}(t) = \sum_j p_j M_j(t)$, which exists for all t. Internally, you keep using mgf-based formulas with X_{approx}, while the calibrated mixture's fat tails ensure that risk measures are much closer to those implied by the original heavy-tailed X than a single normal would be.

Common Mistake: Many candidates conflate finite variance with existence of the mgf, assuming that if $\mathbb{E}[X^2] < \infty$, then $M_X(t)$ exists near 0. For heavy-tailed laws, this is false: polynomially decaying tails can support finite low-order moments but still make $\mathbb{E}[e^{tX}]$ diverge for any $t \neq 0$. Another frequent miss is not distinguishing between matching variance versus matching tail quantiles when proposing an approximate normal-based model for risk.

Chapter 7: Regression and Signal Extraction in Noisy Markets

A trader once joked that the market is like a rock concert recorded on a cheap microphone: the music is in there somewhere, but all you hear at first is noise. This chapter is about learning to separate the music from the static. Linear regression, for all its apparent simplicity, is one of the sharpest tools we have for extracting predictive signals from noisy financial data. It is the workhorse behind a huge fraction of quant trading ideas, from equity factors to intraday microstructure edges, yet it's also one of the easiest models to misuse.

At its core, regression is a way of asking a brutally practical question: "Given what I can observe right now, what should I expect next?" When you regress future returns on today's signals, you are encoding a hypothesis about how the world works. Do cheaper stocks really outperform expensive ones, or is that just a story? Does momentum survive transaction costs, or is it a mirage born of overfitting? Each coefficient in a regression is a miniature answer: if this signal moves by one unit, how much should my expected return move? Interpreting those coefficients correctly is less about algebra and more about skepticism. A positive coefficient is not a license to trade; it is an invitation to ask whether the relationship is robust, stable, and economically meaningful.

One of the curious things about markets is how generous they can be with false patterns. If you throw a dozen signals and a few years of data into a regression, the output will almost always tell you a compelling story. The problem is that markets are high-dimensional and nonstationary: there are many ways to accidentally "explain" the past. Overfitting is what happens when your model becomes an expert in the past and a novice in the future, learning idiosyncrasies of old regimes, rebalance dates, index changes, or even specific corporate events that will never repeat. A model that fits history perfectly can be like a trader who remembers every tick of last year but has no intuition for what matters tomorrow.

Things become even more treacherous when your signals are highly correlated with one another. In practice, most sensible trading signals are cousins: value, quality, and profitability all lean toward similar kinds of stocks; many macro indicators move together with growth and inflation expectations. This multicollinearity can make your regression behave in bizarre ways. Coefficients may flip sign when you add or remove variables, standard errors can explode, and a perfectly reasonable signal can look useless simply because it shares its job with a close relative. Interviewers love probing this point: they will ask why a factor that "everyone knows" works appears insignificant in a multivariate regression, or how you would diagnose and fix spurious coefficient instability in a forecasting model.

From an interviewing standpoint, regression questions are a gold mine. They reveal whether a candidate merely knows formulas or actually understands modeling in a trading context. You might be asked to design a cross-sectional regression to forecast next-month stock returns with a set of factors, and then to critique your own setup: what assumptions did you implicitly make? How do you avoid look-ahead bias? What happens if the signal's predictive power decays over time? Another common line of questioning is about evaluating a trading signal after you've run the regression: how to turn an estimated coefficient into a position size, how to think about t-statistics versus economic significance, or how to benchmark the out-of-sample performance of a signal once it is embedded in a portfolio.

Perhaps the most surprising fact about regression in finance is how far you can get with something so simple. Some of the largest quant shops in the world still lean heavily on linear models for their core signal engines, despite the hype around machine learning. The reasons are practical: regressions are interpretable, fast to update, and diagnostically rich. You can see when relationships weaken, when residuals go haywire, when a new regime seems to break an old edge. In noisy markets, transparency can be a stronger edge than raw complexity.

In the pages that follow, we treat regression not as a piece of classroom statistics, but as a craft for signal extraction under fierce uncertainty. You will see how to set up regressions that forecast returns, how to interpret and stress-test coefficients, how to recognize and mitigate overfitting, and how to navigate the minefield of correlated predictors. Along the way, we will frame these ideas through the kind of problems you are likely to encounter in quant interviews and in real trading research, building an intuition for when to trust a fitted line—and when to suspect that the music you think you hear is just the microphone lying to you.

7.1: Interview Questions

7.1.1: Question 7.1

Question: You are evaluating a new trading signal that predicts next-day excess returns. Historically, only 10% of proposed signals at your firm have true positive expected Sharpe ratio (call these 'good' signals), and 90% are actually noise with zero true Sharpe ('bad' signals).

You run a backtest and obtain an estimated annualized Sharpe of 1.0. Assume: - If a signal is good, its estimated Sharpe from this amount of data is distributed as $N(1.0, 0.5^2)$. - If a signal is bad, its estimated Sharpe is distributed as $N(0.0, 0.5^2)$.

1) Compute (approximately) the posterior probability that this signal is actually good, given the observed estimated Sharpe of 1.0.

2) Intuitively explain why your answer is not as high as many non-quant colleagues might think.

Answer: Let G be "good" and B be "bad." Priors: $P(G) = 0.1$, $P(B) = 0.9$. Likelihoods at Sharpe 1: under G, $N(1, 0.5^2)$ gives density proportional to $\exp(-(1 - 1)^2/(2 \cdot$

$0.5^2)) = 1$. Under B, $N(0, 0.5^2)$ gives density proportional to $\exp(-(1-0)^2/(2 \cdot 0.5^2)) = e^{-2} \approx 0.135$.

By Bayes,

$$P(G \mid \hat{S} = 1) \approx \frac{0.1 \cdot 1}{0.1 \cdot 1 + 0.9 \cdot 0.135} = \frac{0.1}{0.1 + 0.1215} \approx 0.45.$$

Intuition: The result $S \approx 1$ is about 7.4 times more likely if the signal is good than if it is bad, but the prior odds are $1:9$ against being good. Multiplying gives posterior odds about $0.82:1$, i.e., only a $\sim 45\%$ chance it is truly good. Non-quants usually ignore this low base rate and focus only on the impressive-looking Sharpe.

7.1.2: Question 7.2

Question: You monitor a proprietary macro-quant indicator that occasionally flashes "CRISIS" for the next month's equity market. Historically: - True crisis months (large negative market returns) occur with probability 5%. - When a true crisis is coming, the model correctly flashes CRISIS 80% of the time. - When no crisis is coming, the model falsely flashes CRISIS 10% of the time.

1) If the indicator flashes CRISIS this month, what is the probability that a true crisis will actually occur?

2) You now learn that in the last two months, the model flashed CRISIS both times and was wrong both times (no crisis occurred). Assume the model parameters above were actually correct ex ante. How, if at all, should this new information affect your posterior for a CRISIS this month when the indicator flashes again? Explain qualitatively without recalibrating exact numbers.

Answer: For part 1, let C = crisis, N = no crisis, S = CRISIS signal. Using Bayes:

$$P(C \mid S) = \frac{P(S \mid C)P(C)}{P(S \mid C)P(C) + P(S \mid N)P(N)}$$

$$= \frac{0.8 \cdot 0.05}{0.8 \cdot 0.05 + 0.1 \cdot 0.95} = \frac{0.04}{0.135} \approx 0.30.$$

So the probability is about 30%.

For part 2, if you truly believe the given parameters are still correct and fixed, past months are conditionally independent of this month given those parameters, so the two recent false alarms should not change $P(C \mid S)$ at all. If instead you treat the parameters as uncertain, two false positives make you slightly downgrade the model's accuracy, which would modestly lower your posterior crisis probability given a new CRISIS signal.

7.1.3: Question 7.3

Question: You model a stock's daily excess return as
R = β F + ε,
where: - F is a daily market factor return, $F \sim N(0, \sigma\_F^2)$.
- ε is idiosyncratic noise, $\varepsilon \sim N(0, \sigma\_\varepsilon^2)$, independent of F. - β is an unknown factor loading, which you treat as random with prior $\beta \sim N(\beta\_0, \tau^2)$, independent of F and ε.
On a given day, you observe F = f and R = r.

1) Derive (up to proportionality) the posterior distribution of β | (F = f, R = r). You do not need to compute exact closed-form coefficients; just characterize its form and how its mean depends on $(\beta\_0, \tau^2, f, r, \sigma\_\varepsilon^2)$.

2) Provide an intuitive explanation of why observing a larger |f| on that day makes the posterior for β more concentrated (lower variance) than if |f| were small, even if r is the same.

Answer: Conditional on $F = f$ and β, we have $R = \beta f + \varepsilon$, so $R \mid \beta, F = f \sim N(\beta f, \sigma_\varepsilon^2)$. The likelihood in β is proportional to $\exp\{-(r - \beta f)^2/(2\sigma_\varepsilon^2)\}$. The prior is $\beta \sim N(\beta_0, \tau^2)$, proportional to $\exp\{-(\beta - \beta_0)^2/(2\tau^2)\}$. Multiplying, the posterior is Gaussian in β: $\beta \mid (r, f) \sim N(\mu_{\text{post}}, v_{\text{post}})$ with $v_{\text{post}} = 1/(1/\tau^2 + f^2/\sigma_\varepsilon^2)$ and $\mu_{\text{post}} = v_{\text{post}}[\beta_0/\tau^2 + fr/\sigma_\varepsilon^2]$.

Intuition: The data precision term is f^2/σ_ε^2. Larger |f| increases this precision, shrinking v_{post}. A big factor move amplifies the signal βf relative to noise ε, so that day is highly informative about β. When |f| is small, R is mostly noise and hardly updates the prior, leaving a diffuse posterior.

7.1.4: Question 7.4

Question: A quant firm runs 1,000 independent backtests for different trading strategies. For each strategy, they test the null hypothesis H0: "true expected return = 0" using a t-statistic. They decide to greenlight any strategy whose t-statistic exceeds 2 in absolute value.

Suppose the following: - Before seeing the data, you believe only 5% of these strategies truly have non-zero expected return (call these "real" strategies) and 95% are truly zero. - Conditional on being real, a strategy has a 70% chance to produce |t| > 2 in this sample size. - Conditional on being truly zero, a strategy has a 5% chance to produce $|t| > 2$ (i.e., type I error $\approx 5\%$).

1) For a strategy that comes back with $|t| > 2$, what is the posterior probability that it is actually real?

2) Explain how this calculation relates to the notion of "false discovery rate" and why many backtest-driven research processes are overly optimistic if they ignore this base-rate logic.

Answer: Let R = "real," Z = "zero," S = "$|t| > 2$". Given $P(R) = 0.05$, $P(Z) = 0.95$, $P(S \mid R) = 0.70$, $P(S \mid Z) = 0.05$.

By Bayes, $P(R \mid S) = \frac{P(S|R)P(R)}{P(S|R)P(R)+P(S|Z)P(Z)} = \frac{0.70 \cdot 0.05}{0.70 \cdot 0.05 + 0.05 \cdot 0.95} = \frac{0.035}{0.0825} \approx 0.42$.

So even with $|t| > 2$, the chance the strategy is truly real is only about 42%, and $P(Z \mid S) \approx 58\%$. That 58% is the false discovery rate: among "significant" strategies, most are actually null. Ignoring low base rates and multiple testing makes p-values look far more reassuring than they truly are, so backtest-driven research badly overestimates how many greenlit strategies are genuinely profitable.

7.1.5: Question 7.5

Question: You are evaluating a simple daily predictive signal X for next-day return Y. You standardize both variables so that under your model: - Conditional on the signal's true predictive strength θ, the next-day return satisfies $Y = \theta X + \varepsilon$, - $X \sim N(0, 1)$, $\varepsilon \sim N(0, 1)$, independent of each other, - θ is an unknown scalar you treat as random.

You start with a prior $\theta \sim N(0, \sigma_0{}^2)$. You then observe two days of data: (X_1, Y_1) and (X_2, Y_2), assumed independent given θ.

1) Describe how to compute the posterior distribution of θ after observing both days, using a multi-step conditioning argument (first update with day 1, then with day 2). You do not need to write a closed-form expression for every coefficient, but clearly state the structure of the recursion.

2) Suppose $|X_1|$ is very large and $|X_2|$ is very small, and both Y_1 and Y_2 are modest in magnitude. Intuitively, which observation should have more influence on the posterior mean of θ, and why? Connect your answer directly to the conditional variance of Y given X and θ.

Intuition: We have a one-parameter linear-Gaussian model: Y_i is a noisy linear function of X_i with slope θ and fixed noise variance. Gaussian prior plus Gaussian likelihood stays Gaussian, so each new (X_i, Y_i) just updates the mean and variance of θ. The weight each observation gets is driven by how big X_i^2 is relative to the fixed noise variance.

Solution: The model for day i is

$$Y_i = \theta X_i + \varepsilon_i, \quad \varepsilon_i \sim N(0,1), \quad X_i \text{ known.}$$

Thus

$$Y_i \mid \theta, X_i \sim N(\theta X_i, 1).$$

Start with prior

$$\theta \sim N(\mu_0, v_0), \quad \mu_0 = 0, \quad v_0 = \sigma_0^2.$$

Update with day 1. The posterior after observing (X_1, Y_1) is Gaussian:

$$\theta \mid X_1, Y_1 \sim N(\mu_1, v_1),$$

with precision (inverse variance) adding:

$$\frac{1}{v_1} = \frac{1}{v_0} + X_1^2,$$

so

$$v_1 = \frac{1}{\dfrac{1}{v_0} + X_1^2},$$

and mean

$$\mu_1 = v_1 \left(\frac{\mu_0}{v_0} + X_1 Y_1 \right).$$

Since $\mu_0 = 0$, this becomes

$$\mu_1 = v_1 X_1 Y_1.$$

Now treat this posterior as the new prior and update with day 2. With prior $\theta \sim N(\mu_1, v_1)$ and likelihood $Y_2 \mid \theta, X_2 \sim N(\theta X_2, 1)$, the new posterior is

$$\theta \mid X_1, Y_1, X_2, Y_2 \sim N(\mu_2, v_2),$$

with

$$\frac{1}{v_2} = \frac{1}{v_1} + X_2^2, \quad v_2 = \frac{1}{\dfrac{1}{v_1} + X_2^2},$$

and

$$\mu_2 = v_2 \left(\frac{\mu_1}{v_1} + X_2 Y_2 \right).$$

In recursive form for $i = 1,2$:

$$\frac{1}{v_i} = \frac{1}{v_{i-1}} + X_i^2, \quad v_i = \frac{1}{\dfrac{1}{v_{i-1}} + X_i^2},$$

$$\mu_i = v_i \left(\frac{\mu_{i-1}}{v_{i-1}} + X_i Y_i \right).$$

The algorithmic logic is: start from (μ_0, v_0); for each (X_i, Y_i), you add X_i^2 to the precision and add $X_i Y_i$ to the precision-weighted mean, then invert to get the new variance and multiply to get the new mean.

Common Mistake: A common mistake is to think both days are equally informative because the noise variance of Y is always 1. In fact, the informativeness about θ depends on X_i. From

$$Y_i \mid \theta, X_i \sim N(\theta X_i, 1),$$

the variance of Y_i around its mean is always 1, but the sensitivity of the mean to θ is X_i. The Fisher information and the precision update both scale with X_i^2. When $|X_1|$ is large, changing θ noticeably shifts θX_1, so Y_1 is highly informative about θ. When $|X_2|$ is tiny, $\theta X_2 \approx 0$ for any plausible θ, so Y_2 is almost pure noise with respect to θ.

This appears directly in the updates: X_1^2 enters the precision strongly, shrinking v_1 a lot and making μ_1 (and thus μ_2) heavily influenced by Y_1. In contrast, X_2^2 contributes almost nothing to $1/v_2$, so the second day barely moves the posterior. Hence, the first observation with large $|X_1|$ should dominate the posterior mean of θ.

7.1.6: Question 7.6

Question: You are modeling daily P&L of a high-frequency strategy. Empirically, you observe: - Mean close to zero. - Variance roughly stable over time. - Occasional 8–10 standard deviation moves relative to the sample standard deviation. - The sign of large moves is roughly symmetric (big gains and big losses both occur).

1) Argue, using moment and tail considerations rather than "eyeballing histograms," why a normal distribution is likely a poor model here.

2) Propose a more suitable parametric family among: (a) Normal, (b) Student t, (c) Skew-normal, (d) Lognormal. Justify your choice by discussing how its kurtosis and tail behavior differ from the normal and how that affects risk estimates like VaR.

3) Suppose you fit both a normal and a Student t to the same data and both match the sample variance. Explain qualitatively how the 99% one-day VaR estimate will differ between the two models, and why this difference arises even though the variances are matched.

Answer: Under a true normal with variance $sigma^2$, 8–10σ moves have vanishing probability; seeing them with non-negligible frequency implies strong excess kurtosis and much fatter tails than a Gaussian, so the normal severely understates tail risk even though it matches mean and variance. A Student t is most suitable: it is symmetric like the P&L, unlike lognormal; it has polynomially decaying, heavy tails and excess kurtosis, unlike normal and skew-normal, so it can generate frequent large moves. This fatter tail puts much more probability mass beyond extreme quantiles. If both normal and t match the same variance, the 99% VaR from the t will be more negative: to keep variance fixed while thickening tails, probability shifts from the center to extremes, pushing the 1% and 99% quantiles further from zero.

7.1.7: Question 7.7

Question: You are deciding whether to model a stock's daily arithmetic return R directly, or to model its daily log-return L = log(1 + R). You are told that over the horizon of interest, R is rarely below -5% and rarely above +5%, and that a lognormal model for prices is a reasonable approximation.

1) Using a Taylor expansion or moment-based argument, explain why modeling L as approximately normal often leads to more stable estimates of expectation and variance than modeling R as normal.

2) Under a lognormal price model, daily log-returns L are exactly normal, and arithmetic returns are R = e^L - 1. Describe how the skewness of R arises even though L is symmetric, and what this implies for the distribution of large gains vs large losses.

3) In a regression of next-day return on signals, explain one statistical advantage (and one potential drawback) of working with log-returns instead of arithmetic returns when you later aggregate predictions over multiple days.

Answer: For small R, $L = \log(1 + R) \approx R - R^2/2$. The $-R^2/2$ term partially removes the effect of large $|R|$, making L closer to homoskedastic and approximately normal; its mean and variance are more stable across time and price levels than those of R, whose Gaussian model also incorrectly allows $R < -1$.

If $L \sim N(\mu, \sigma^2)$, then $R = e^L - 1$ is a convex transform of a symmetric variable. The exponential stretches the right tail and the left tail is bounded at -1, so R is positively skewed: very large gains are more probable than equally large losses.

In regressions, log-returns add over days, so multi-day forecasts and variances combine linearly, which is a major advantage. A drawback is that mapping predicted L back to R via $e^L - 1$ is nonlinear, so arithmetic returns and P&L are less directly interpretable and simple exponentiation of predicted means is biased for expected arithmetic returns.

7.1.8: Question 7.8

Question: You suspect the daily returns of an asset follow a simple two-regime mixture model: - With probability p, the market is in a "calm" regime: $R \mid$ calm $\sim N(\mu_c, \sigma_c^2)$. - With probability $1 - p$, the market is in a "volatile" regime: $R \mid$ volatile $\sim N(\mu_v, \sigma_v^2)$, with $\sigma_v^2 \gg \sigma_c^2$. Regimes are i.i.d. across days and unobserved.

1) Express $E[R]$ and $\mathrm{Var}(R)$ in terms of $p, \mu_c, \mu_v, \sigma_c^2, \sigma_v^2$, and separate within-regime vs. between-regime variance.

2) Assume $\mu_c = \mu_v = \mu$. Explain how rare volatile days affect higher moments and tails vs. a single $N(\mu, \sigma^2)$ with the same variance.

3) You fit a single normal with mean $\hat{\mu}$ and variance $\hat{\sigma}^2$. Explain qualitatively why this underestimates large drawdown risk, even if $\hat{\sigma}^2 = \mathrm{Var}(R)$.

Intuition: The mixture is "sometimes calm, sometimes wild." The mean is just the average of regime means. The variance has two pieces: average volatility inside regimes, plus extra variance because the mean shifts when the regime changes. Even if overall variance matches a single Gaussian, the mixture packs more mass near the center on calm days and pushes the "saved" probability into very fat tails on volatile days. A single normal spreads risk smoothly every day, so it misses these rare blow-ups.

Solution: Using the law of total expectation,

$$E[R] = E(E[R \mid \text{regime}]) = p\mu_c + (1-p)\mu_v.$$

For the variance, use the law of total variance:

$$\text{Var}(R) = E(\text{Var}(R \mid \text{regime})) + \text{Var}(E[R \mid \text{regime}]).$$

First term (within-regime variance):

$$E(\text{Var}(R \mid \text{regime})) = p\sigma_c^2 + (1-p)\sigma_v^2.$$

Let $M = E[R \mid \text{regime}]$, so $M = \mu_c$ with prob p, μ_v with prob $1 - p$. Then

$$\text{Var}(M) = p(\mu_c - E[R])^2 + (1-p)(\mu_v - E[R])^2.$$

This is the between-regime contribution:

$$\text{Var}(R) = p\sigma_c^2 + (1-p)\sigma_v^2$$

within regimes

$$+ p(\mu_c - E[R])^2 + (1-p)(\mu_v - E[R])^2.$$

variation in means

If $\mu_c = \mu_v = \mu$, then $E[R] = \mu$ and

$$\text{Var}(E[R \mid \text{regime}]) = 0, \quad \text{Var}(R) = p\sigma_c^2 + (1-p)\sigma_v^2.$$

But the distribution is a mixture of a narrow $N(\mu, \sigma_c^2)$ and a very wide $N(\mu, \sigma_v^2)$. To match the same variance, a single $N(\mu, \sigma^2)$ must choose an intermediate σ^2. The mixture has most probability very close to μ on calm days plus rare huge moves from the volatile regime, so its kurtosis is higher and tails are fatter than any single Gaussian with that same σ^2.

Logic: A single fitted normal with $\hat{\mu} \approx \mu$ and $\hat{\sigma}^2 \approx \text{Var}(R)$ assumes identical volatility every day. In reality, most days are less risky than $\hat{\sigma}$ (calm regime), but a small fraction are much more dangerous (volatile regime). The Gaussian fit smooths this and under-allocates probability to very large moves. Over multiple days, paths containing one or a few volatile days dominate drawdowns. The single normal model, lacking regime shifts, understates how often these extreme paths occur, so it understates the likelihood and severity of large drawdowns.

Common Mistake: Candidates often stop at $p\sigma_c^2 + (1 - p)\sigma_v^2$ and forget the $\text{Var}(E[R \mid \text{regime}])$ term, or they claim matching variance implies similar tail risk, missing that mixtures with equal variance can still have much heavier tails than a single normal.

7.1.9: Question 7.9

Question: Two strategies A and B both trade once per day and have the same sample mean daily return and the same sample standard deviation over several years. However, their empirical return distributions differ: - Strategy A's returns look roughly normal. - Strategy B's returns appear heavy-tailed: many small moves, but occasional very large positive or negative days.

    1) Explain how these two strategies can have the same sample Sharpe ratio while having very different

higher moments. Why does the Sharpe ratio fail to distinguish their tail risk profiles?

2) Suppose you must choose a parametric family for each: you consider Gaussian for A and Student t for B, both calibrated to the same mean and variance as their sample data. Qualitatively compare the estimated probability of a daily loss worse than -4 standard deviations under each fitted model.

3) Discuss how the presence of heavy tails in B affects the reliability (sampling distribution) of its estimated Sharpe ratio compared to A, even if they have the same true mean and variance.

Answer: The Sharpe ratio uses only mean and variance, $SR = \mu/\sigma$. If A and B share the same sample μ and σ, they have the same sample Sharpe, regardless of skewness or kurtosis. Thus, it ignores how risk is distributed in the tails. With A modeled as Gaussian, $P(R < -4\sigma)$ is tiny, about 10^{-5}–10^{-6}. For B, a Student t with the same μ and σ has much heavier tails, so $P(R < -4\sigma)$ is orders of magnitude larger, reflecting far more tail risk.

Heavy tails in B create more frequent large outliers, making its sample mean and variance unstable. Therefore its estimated Sharpe has a wider, more erratic sampling distribution than A's, even if their true Sharpe ratios are identical.

7.1.10: Question 7.10

Question: You are evaluating a portfolio of two independent quant strategies, X and Y, each trading different markets. You observe that: - $E[X] = E[Y] = \mu > 0$,

Var(X) = Var(Y) = σ^2. - X is approximately normal. - Y is heavy-tailed with finite variance σ^2 but much higher kurtosis than a normal. Assume X and Y are independent.

1) Compare the distribution of the portfolio return P = X + Y to that of 2X (i.e., doubling capital in strategy X). Both have the same mean and variance. Qualitatively, which has heavier tails, and why?

2) As you add more independent copies of Y (Y_1, Y_2, ..., Y_n), each with the same heavy-tailed distribution and finite variance, consider their standardized sum $S\_n = (Y_1 + ... + Y\_n - n\mu) / (\sigma\sqrt{n})$. Describe how the central limit theorem applies here and what it implies about the *shape* of S_n for moderate n, not just as n → ∞.

3) In practice, suppose you build a portfolio that mixes many nearly normal strategies and a few heavy-tailed ones like Y. Explain why matching only the overall portfolio mean and variance to a target may still leave you exposed to unexpected tail risk, and how understanding the distributional types (normal vs heavy-tailed) of components helps in stress testing and risk control.

Answer: For part 1, both $P = X + Y$ and $2X$ have mean 2μ and variance $2\sigma^2$, but P is heavier-tailed because Y is heavy-tailed; in the extremes, large realizations of Y dominate, while $2X$ remains a thin-tailed normal scaled by 2.

For part 2, the CLT applies since $\mathrm{Var}(Y)$ is finite, so $S_n \Rightarrow N(0,1)$ as $n \to \infty$. For moderate n, convergence in the center is faster than in the tails, so S_n still has noticeably fatter tails and higher peak than a true standard normal.

For part 3, matching only mean and variance ignores tail shape. A few Y-type strategies can dominate extreme losses even with small variance share. Knowing which legs are heavy-tailed guides targeted stress tests, tighter limits, and de-levering of those components to control tail risk beyond variance.

Chapter 8: Time Series, Dependence Over Time, and Practical Interview Drills

If you have ever stared at a price chart and felt that yesterday's move was somehow "still in the air" today, you've already intuited the heart of this chapter: dependence over time. In cross-sectional statistics, we typically imagine drawing data points like marbles from a giant urn—each independent of the last. Time series laughs at that picture. Markets remember. Not perfectly, not forever, and often in deceptive ways. But they remember enough that exploiting, understanding, or at least not being fooled by this memory is central to quantitative work.

Here we step into that world without burying you in heavy machinery. Rather than start with intimidating notation, we'll build intuition: how a current value can be expressed as a nudge from the past plus a bit of new randomness, how shocks echo and then fade, and why clusters of calm days can suddenly erupt into storms of volatility. As you will see, time dependence doesn't need to be mystical. It can often be framed in simple stories: "today equals a fraction of yesterday plus noise," or "tomorrow's regime depends on where we are now."

One of the most striking empirical regularities in finance is volatility clustering. Prices themselves can look nearly random, but their variability does not. Quiet days tend to follow quiet days; tumult clusters together too. This pattern was noticed long before modern econometrics existed—early commodity traders observed "periods of excitement" followed by relative lulls. Today, this observation underpins entire risk-management frameworks: the same VaR model that looks fine in a tranquil month explodes in error when a volatility cluster arrives. Interviewers love to probe whether a candidate has internalized this: Can you articulate why squared returns are more predictable than returns? Can you reason through how a shock today changes the distribution of tomorrow's risk, even if it doesn't reveal an obvious trading edge?

We'll also explore simple Markov models, which formalize the idea that the future can depend on the present in a structured, probabilistic way. For a first cut, you can imagine a market that flips between a "calm" regime and a "turbulent" regime, each with its own volatility level. The rule that governs transitions—how likely you are to move from calm to turbulent tomorrow if you're calm today—is a Markov dynamic. Surprisingly, even two-state toy models like this are rich enough to capture essential phenomena: regime switches, skewed risk, and path-dependent P&L outcomes that matter a lot for trading desks and risk teams. Throughout the chapter, we'll keep our tools deliberately light. Think AR/MA-style reasoning—current values expressed as linear functions of past values and past shocks—without diving into deep time-series theory. The emphasis is on building your instinct: how a small modification in the dependence structure changes persistence, predictability, and risk. For instance, if you tweak an autoregressive parameter slightly upwards, how does that alter the "memory" of the process and its long-run variability? If innovations become more volatile but less persistent, what happens to drawdowns, or to the Sharpe ratio of a simple strategy?

To turn these ideas from abstract concepts into tools you can use under pressure, we close the chapter with a consolidated set of interview-style drills. These problems braid together time dependence, basic probability, and classical statistics in settings that mirror what you'll face in quant interviews and on the desk. You might be asked to reason about a P&L process with Markovian regimes, to detect volatility clustering using simple statistics, or to infer whether a strategy's backtest is likely overfitting independent noise or genuinely exploiting a temporal pattern.

One curious fact you'll see emerge is that even "useless" models can be valuable. An oversimplified AR(1) or two-state Markov model almost never describes reality in full, yet it can sharpen your sense for what features in the data actually matter—and which are illusions. Another is that many apparently sophisticated trading signals reduce, under the hood, to very simple temporal structures: mean reversion, momentum, or regime dependence, dressed up with complex language.

By the end of this chapter, you should be able to look at a time-ordered dataset and immediately start asking the

143

right questions: Where is the memory? How does risk propagate through time? Which simple dynamics could plausibly generate what I see? And crucially, can I communicate that reasoning clearly and rapidly when someone across the table says, "Walk me through your intuition"?

8.1: Interview Questions

8.1.1: Question 8.1

Question: Given a financial time series exhibiting volatility clustering, how would you model the conditional variance to capture periods of high and low volatility?

Answer: Use a GARCH-type specification for the conditional variance. Let returns be $r_t = \mu_t + \varepsilon_t$ with $\varepsilon_t = \sigma_t z_t$ and z_t i.i.d. with mean 0 and variance 1. A basic GARCH(1,1) for the conditional variance is $\sigma_t^2 = \omega + \alpha \varepsilon_{t-1}^2 + \beta \sigma_{t-1}^2$, with $\omega > 0$, $\alpha \geq 0$, $\beta \geq 0$, and $\alpha + \beta < 1$. Past shocks ε_{t-1}^2 and past variance σ_{t-1}^2 drive current volatility, capturing clustering. For asymmetry or leverage effects, extend to EGARCH or GJR-GARCH.

8.1.2: Question 8.2

Question: How can coarse-graining of Markov chains be applied to detect synchronization clusters in multivariate time series?

Intuition: For a multivariate time series from many interacting units, exact phase-space dynamics are high-dimensional and noisy. Instead of tracking detailed continuous states, you encode the dynamics as a Markov chain over symbolic states and then merge states that behave similarly. When you coarse-grain in a way that preserves the essential transition structure, groups of components that evolve in a coordinated fashion naturally form "blocks" or modules in the Markov chain. These blocks correspond to synchronization clusters.

Solution: Start with M time series, for example phases $\phi_i(t), i = 1, \dots, M$. Define a symbolic state $s(t)$ that encodes the joint configuration at time t, such as

$$s(t) = (b_1(t), \dots, b_M(t)),$$

where $b_i(t)$ is a discrete bin of $\phi_i(t)$ or of some phase-difference feature. The sequence $\{s(t)\}$ is modeled as a Markov chain with transition matrix

$$P_{ab} = \Pr(s(t+1) = b \mid s(t) = a).$$

Synchronization implies that certain components change their symbols together, so states that differ only within such a synchronized group will have very similar outgoing transition distributions. Coarse-graining means defining a partition $\mathcal{C} = \{C_1, \dots, C_K\}$ of the original state space such that all $a \in C_k$ have nearly identical rows $P_{a\cdot}$. The coarse-grained chain has states C_k with transitions

$$\tilde{P}_{kl} = \frac{1}{\mu(C_k)} \sum_{a \in C_k} \sum_{b \in C_l} \mu(a) P_{ab},$$

where μ is the stationary distribution. The partition is chosen to minimize information loss, for example by minimizing a divergence between the original and coarse-grained dynamics.

Because synchronized subsystems induce low-dimensional, nearly Markovian dynamics, the optimal coarse-graining groups microstates according to which subset of variables moves together. Reading off which components change coherently within each coarse-grained state identifies synchronization clusters.

Logic: Construct symbolic dynamics from the multivariate signal, estimate the Markov matrix, then apply an information-theoretic or spectral partitioning that merges states with similar transition patterns. Interpret each robust module in the coarse-grained chain as a synchronization cluster of the underlying variables.

Common Mistake: Candidates often only cluster time series by pairwise correlation and ignore the transition structure. Without using how states evolve probabilistically, they miss clusters that are synchronized in dynamics but not strongly correlated instantaneously.

8.1.3: Question 8.3

Question: Explain the process of determining the appropriate order for an Autoregressive (AR) model in time series analysis.

Answer: To choose the AR order p, first ensure the series is stationary (often via differencing or transformations). Then examine the ACF and PACF. For a pure AR(p) process, the PACF shows a sharp cutoff after lag p, while the ACF decays gradually. The lag where PACF coefficients become statistically insignificant (e.g., outside confidence bounds) gives an initial estimate of p. Next, fit several AR models with different p (around that estimate) and compare them using information criteria such as AIC or BIC. The preferred order is the one with the lowest AIC/BIC, balancing goodness-of-fit against model complexity.

8.1.4: Question 8.4

Question: You are tracking whether a daily trading signal is currently in a 'good regime' (G) or a 'bad regime' (B). At the start of today, based on past performance you believe $P(G) = 0.3$ and $P(B) = 0.7$.

Each day the signal outputs either +1 (long) or -1 (short). Historically, in regime G the signal is correct about the next-day return direction 70% of the time, while in regime B it is correct only 55% of the time. Assume that conditional on the regime, daily calls are independent over time.

    (a) Today the signal says +1 and the next-day return is indeed positive. Compute your updated posterior probability that the signal is in regime G.

    (b) Intuitively, explain why seeing several correct calls in a row does *not* necessarily mean your posterior will eventually be close to 1, even though G is strictly better than B.

Answer: For part (a), let C be "today's call is correct." By Bayes' rule, $P(G \mid C) = \frac{P(C|G)P(G)}{P(C|G)P(G)+P(C|B)P(B)} = \frac{0.7 \cdot 0.3}{0.7 \cdot 0.3+0.55 \cdot 0.7} = \frac{0.21}{0.595} \approx 0.354.$

Intuition: For part (b), both regimes can easily produce streaks of correct calls, since even in B the signal is correct 55% of the time. The likelihood ratio after k correct calls is

$(0.7/0.55)^k$, which grows slowly because 0.7 and 0.55 are close. Starting from prior odds 0.3/0.7, many correct calls are needed before the evidence strongly overwhelms the prior; until then, the posterior can remain far from 1.

8.1.5: Question 8.5

Question: You are comparing two intraday strategies, A and B. Historically: - Strategy A is active on 10% of days and, when active, has a 65% chance of making money that day. - Strategy B is active on 50% of days and, when active, has a 58% chance of making money.

You only know the P&L series is equally likely a priori to be A or B. You observe that over the last 4 days, the strategy was active all 4 days and made money on 3 of them.

(a) Compute the posterior probability that the series comes from strategy B.

(b) Explain the main intuition behind why the posterior favors one strategy over the other, despite A having a higher conditional success rate when active.

Answer: Let E be "active 4 days, profitable on 3." $P(E \mid A) = 0.1^4 \binom{4}{3} 0.65^3 0.35$ and $P(E \mid B) = 0.5^4 \binom{4}{3} 0.58^3 0.42$.

With equal priors, $P(B \mid E) = \frac{P(E|B)}{P(E|A)+P(E|B)}$. The ratio

$$\frac{P(E|B)}{P(E|A)} = \frac{0.5^4}{0.1^4} \left(\frac{0.58}{0.65}\right)^3 \frac{0.42}{0.35} \approx 5^4 \times 0.71 \times 1.2 \approx 5.3 \times 10^2, \quad \text{so}$$

$P(B \mid E) \approx \frac{532}{533} \approx 0.998$.

Intuition: Four consecutive active days are incredibly unlikely for A ($0.1^4 = 0.0001$) but quite plausible for B ($0.5^4 = 0.0625$). This massive difference in activity frequency dominates the small edge in A's conditional win rate (65% vs 58%), so the data overwhelmingly point to B.

8.1.6: Question 8.6

Question: You are monitoring whether a newly deployed alpha is genuinely profitable. Model each day's sign of excess return as either coming from a 'null' model N (no edge, pure noise) or an 'edge' model E (positive edge). Under N, daily sign is +1 or -1 with equal probability 0.5. Under E, the probability of +1 is 0.6 and -1 is 0.4. Assume conditional independence of days given the model.

    (a) You start with prior $P(E) = 0.2$, $P(N) = 0.8$. Over the first 3 days you observe the sequence of signs: +1, +1, -1. Compute the posterior probability $P(E \mid data\_3)$.

    (b) Now suppose that, independent of the data, your risk committee imposes a time-decay on the prior to reflect that new alphas tend to decay quickly: at the start of each new day t, before seeing that day's sign, your prior $P\_t(E)$ is shrunk halfway towards 0.1 according to

$P\_t(E) = 0.1 + 0.5 \times (P\_{t-1}(E) - 0.1)$.

Then you update with Bayes' rule using day t's sign.

Compute $P\_4(E \mid$ data up to day 4) if day 4's sign is +1, starting from your answer in (a) for day 3. (You may keep intermediate values as decimals.)

    (c) Conceptually, what is this prior-shrinkage doing to your long-run belief about the alpha, even if you keep seeing mostly positive signs? How is this different from standard Bayesian updating without such a mechanism?

Intuition: You are comparing two hypotheses: "no edge" versus "edge." Each day's sign is evidence that slightly favors one model. Bayes' rule combines how likely the observed signs are under each model with your prior belief in each model. In part (b), the committee forces you to repeatedly "forget" some of your accumulated confidence, pulling beliefs back toward a low base rate that alphas persist.

Solution: For part (a), let the data be

$$D_3 = \{+1, +1, -1\}.$$

Under N each sign has probability 0.5, so

$$P(D_3 \mid N) = 0.5 \times 0.5 \times 0.5 = 0.5^3 = 0.125.$$

Under E,

$$P(+1 \mid E) = 0.6, \quad P(-1 \mid E) = 0.4,$$

so

$$P(D_3 \mid E) = 0.6 \times 0.6 \times 0.4 = 0.144.$$

With prior $P(E) = 0.2$, $P(N) = 0.8$, Bayes' rule gives

$$P(E \mid D_3) = \frac{P(D_3 \mid E)P(E)}{P(D_3 \mid E)P(E) + P(D_3 \mid N)P(N)}$$

$$= \frac{0.144 \cdot 0.2}{0.144 \cdot 0.2 + 0.125 \cdot 0.8}.$$

Compute numerator and denominator:

$$\text{num} = 0.144 \times 0.2 = 0.0288,$$

$$\text{den} = 0.0288 + 0.125 \times 0.8 = 0.0288 + 0.1 = 0.1288.$$

So

$$P(E \mid D_3) \approx \frac{0.0288}{0.1288} \approx 0.2236.$$

For part (b), denote

$$p_3 = P_3(E \mid \text{data up to day 3}) \approx 0.2236.$$

Before seeing day 4, you apply shrinkage:

$$P_4^{\text{prior}}(E) = 0.1 + 0.5(p_3 - 0.1) = 0.1 + 0.5(0.2236 - 0.1)$$
$$= 0.1 + 0.0618 = 0.1618.$$

Thus $P_4^{\text{prior}}(N) = 1 - 0.1618 = 0.8382$.

Day 4 sign is $+1$. Likelihoods for a single $+1$ are

$$P(+1 \mid E) = 0.6, \quad P(+1 \mid N) = 0.5.$$

Update again with Bayes:

$$P_4(E \mid \text{data up to day 4}) = \frac{0.6 \cdot 0.1618}{0.6 \cdot 0.1618 + 0.5 \cdot 0.8382}.$$

Compute:

$$\text{num} = 0.6 \times 0.1618 = 0.09708,$$
$$\text{den} = 0.09708 + 0.5 \times 0.8382 = 0.09708 + 0.4191$$
$$= 0.51618.$$

So

$$P_4(E \mid \text{data up to day 4}) \approx \frac{0.09708}{0.51618} \approx 0.188.$$

Notice this is actually lower than 0.2236, even after a positive day, because the forced shrinkage reduced the prior so much.

For part (c), the shrinkage rule acts like mean reversion of your belief toward 0.1. Even with many positive days, every new day you are partially "reset" toward low confidence that the edge persists. The data try to push $P(E)$ up, but the mechanism continuously drags it back, so your belief tends to stabilize around some intermediate level rather than converging to 1.

In standard Bayesian updating without this mechanism, the prior is only set once. If you keep observing evidence favoring E, the posterior $P(E \mid \text{data})$ would monotonically increase and could get arbitrarily close to 1 as data accumulate. Here, by contrast, you have an explicit model of nonstationarity or alpha decay: even strong recent evidence cannot fully overcome the built-in expectation that edges die out, so long-run certainty about a permanent edge is structurally prevented.

8.1.7: Question 8.7

Question: You classify each trading day as either 'high-vol' (H) or 'low-vol' (L) using a noisy indicator. The true regime follows a two-state Markov chain: - P(H tomorrow | H today) = 0.9, P(L tomorrow | H today) = 0.1 - P(H tomorrow | L today) = 0.2, P(L tomorrow | L today) = 0.8 Your indicator each day outputs "H" or "L". Conditional on the true regime that day, it is correct with probability 0.8 and incorrect with probability 0.2.

Assume that at the start of day 1, your belief is P(true H on day 1) = 0.5.

You then observe the following indicator outputs: - Day 1: H - Day 2: H

(a) Compute the posterior probability that the true regime on day 2 is H, using correct multi-step conditioning (you must account for the Markov transition and the noisy observations).

(b) Briefly explain the roles played by the Markov dependence and the observation noise in shaping your posterior.

Answer: For part (a), let X_t be the true regime and Y_t the indicator. First update day 1: $P(X_1 = H \mid Y_1 = H) \propto 0.8 \cdot$

$0.5 = 0.4$, $P(X_1 = L \mid Y_1 = H) \propto 0.2 \cdot 0.5 = 0.1$, so $P(X_1 = H \mid Y_1 = H) = 0.8$, $P(X_1 = L \mid Y_1 = H) = 0.2$.

Predict day 2 before Y_2: $P(X_2 = H \mid Y_1 = H) = 0.9 \cdot 0.8 + 0.2 \cdot 0.2 = 0.76$, $P(X_2 = L \mid Y_1 = H) = 0.24$.

Incorporate $Y_2 = H$: $\tilde{P}_H = 0.8 \cdot 0.76 = 0.608$, $\tilde{P}_L = 0.2 \cdot 0.24 = 0.048$, $P(X_2 = H \mid Y_1 = H, Y_2 = H) = 0.608/(0.608 + 0.048) \approx 0.927$.

For part (b), Markov dependence makes regimes persistent, so an H on day 1 raises the prior chance of H on day 2 even before Y_2. Observation noise (80% accuracy) means each H signal is only partial evidence; two consistent noisy H's, combined with high persistence, push the posterior close to but below 1.

8.1.8: Question 8.8

Question: You are evaluating a binary predictive signal for next-day stock returns. Under the null hypothesis H0 (no predictive power), the signal is equally likely to be 'up' or 'down', independent of the next-day return. Under the alternative H1 (predictive power), the signal is 'up' with probability 0.7 on days when the return is positive, and 'up' with probability 0.3 on days when the return is negative. Assume P(positive return) = P(negative return) = 0.5 under both hypotheses.

You start with prior odds P(H1) : P(H0) = 1 : 9.

Over the next 5 days, you observe that on 4 days the signal says 'up' and the return is positive, and on 1 day the signal says 'up' and the return is negative. (There are no 'down' signals in this short sample.) Assume days are independent given the hypothesis.

    (a) Compute the likelihood ratio L = P(data | H1) / P(data | H0).

    (b) Compute the posterior odds P(H1 | data) : P(H0 | data) and the posterior probability P(H1 | data).

    (c) Explain why this amount of evidence is still relatively weak, despite 4 out of 5 'up' signals being correct.

Answer: Under H_0, each observed day type has probability $0.5 \times 0.5 = 0.25$, so $P(D \mid H_0) \propto 0.25^5$.

Under H_1, a (up, positive) day has probability $0.5 \times 0.7 = 0.35$ and a (up, negative) day $0.5 \times 0.3 = 0.15$, so $P(D \mid H_1) \propto 0.35^4 \cdot 0.15$.

Thus $L = \frac{P(D|H_1)}{P(D|H_0)} = \frac{0.35^4 \cdot 0.15}{0.25^5} \approx 2.3$.

Posterior odds are prior odds times L: $P(H_1 \mid D) : P(H_0 \mid D) = 1 \cdot 2.3 : 9 \approx 2.3 : 9$.

So $P(H_1 \mid D) = \frac{2.3}{2.3 + 9} \approx 0.20$.

Intuition: Under H_0 you already expect about 50% correct by chance, and with only 5 days, seeing 4 correct is not that rare. The data are only about 2.3 times more likely under H_1, which is modest evidence; starting from a skeptical 10% prior, you only move to about 20% belief in H_1.